Dear Haddad Family,
May you find inspiration and spiritual strength within these pages.
God bless you!
Paul Dykewicz

HOLY SMOKES!

Golden Guidance from
Notre Dame's Championship Chaplain

PAUL DYKEWICZ

Xulon PRESS

DEDICATION

I want to thank everyone who aided and encouraged me on my multi-year adventure of reporting, researching and writing this book about the inspirational life and guidance of Notre Dame's championship chaplain, Fr. James Riehle. My mother, Evelyn, and late father, Richard, deserve blessings from heaven for raising me with love to pursue my dreams. My sister, Clare, brother Philip, brother Mark and sister-in-law Lenora have provided me with much appreciated support. My nephews Stuart, Duncan, Matthew and William motivate me to leave lasting lessons to benefit future generations.

Former University of Notre Dame Presidents Theodore Hesburgh and Edward "Monk" Malloy provided great stories and insights. John Heisler, Carol Copley and their colleagues in the Notre Dame Athletics Department helped in many ways, as did the university's Monogram Club leaders of the past and present who included Jim Fraleigh, Beth Hunter, Marty Allen, Haley (Scott) DeMaria and Reggie Brooks. In addition, thanks to the more than 100 sources for this book.

Special thanks to those who provided photographs, especially Michael and Susan Bennett, of Lighthouse Imaging, and the University of Notre Dame Athletics Department. James and Jeannine Ruse, Fr. Riehle's nephew and niece, supplied family photos that included the one of their wedding at the front of Chapter 4 that features their "Uncle Jim" as the priest.

Gratitude also goes to the men and women who took part in creating the rich tradition at the University of Notre Dame, which I began to appreciate early in my childhood. I loved to play with my dad's Notre Dame football and enjoyed scoring countless touchdowns as I pretended to be a Fighting Irish running back who refused to stop short of crossing the goal line. I never fulfilled that dream of athletic stardom but the Lord deserves the ultimate thanks for finding a special role for me as the author of this book.

TABLE OF CONTENTS

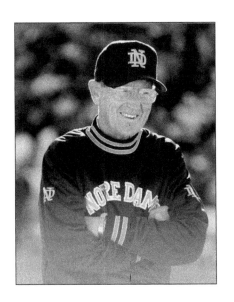

FOREWORD
By Lou Holtz

Each of us ideally should have someone in our lives whom we can count on to guide us through the toughest times, as well as to help us to enjoy our successes. Fr. James Riehle was just such a person for students, athletes, coaches, administrators, support staffers and many others at the University of Notre Dame for an eventful four decades. His tenure began during the Vietnam War era in the 1960s and extended to the earliest years of the new millennium. Fr. Riehle shared a unique sense of humor, along with good judgment, excellent listening skills and motivational words. As a former salesman who did not become a clergyman until he was almost 40 years old, Fr. Riehle had a wealth of real-world experience that aided him in assisting others to overcome adversity and fulfill their potential.

I was among those fortunate enough to have Fr. Riehle as a friend and a confidant. But he also played a pivotal, behind-the-scenes role in the lives of a large number of people. He would speak the truth, help you to enjoy life and use humor to break the tension of pressure-packed situations. Fr. Riehle was a true legend at Notre Dame but he never sought the limelight or any accolades for himself. He first and foremost was a clergyman who served the Lord and tried to be available whenever others needed him.

Anyone who ever watched the movie *Rudy* saw Fr. Riehle in action as he played himself when reciting a pre-game prayer. Fr. Riehle also appeared in a television commercial with Joe Montana, who later won four Super Bowls and gained induction into the Pro Football Hall of Fame. But those instances of public recognition did not change Fr. Riehle in the least. He performed his duties ably and humbly. He also became popular among time-crunched students on campus for his quick but meaningful Masses and homilies.

If you think a priest might not make much of a difference to a team, its players or coaches, you didn't know Fr. Riehle. He was a star performer even though he never made an All American team, scored a touchdown or won a Heisman Trophy. But he certainly helped those who reached those lofty heights. In fact, he was the football team's chaplain for two national championships in 1966 and 1973 during the legendary tenure of Ara Parseghian, one with Dan Devine in 1977 and another with me in 1988 when I served as Notre Dame's football coach. Championship seasons are special and do not think for a second that Fr. Riehle was not a key part of the success of those teams. His inspiring prayer in the locker room after a brief pre-game brawl with the University of Miami team in 1988 re-focused the players on the game, fired up everyone listening to him and prepared all of us for a classic contest that went down to the last play. Without Fr. Riehle, I don't know if we would have won that game between two previously unbeaten teams, finished the season with a perfect record and become the national champions. His contributions were that important to us. I still treasure the religious medals that he gave to each of us who attended pre-game Masses with him.

If you had a problem and needed instant wisdom from someone to help you, Fr. Riehle was about the best choice you could find. When disappointments occurred, Fr. Riehle could console you but also aid you in preparing to give your best effort the next time. In sports, a saying exists that you don't want to let the same team beat you twice. You can lose once on the field of play but you need to be able to move beyond the setback and prepare yourself to win the next game. Fr. Riehle was a master motivator and a tough competitor himself who understood the kind of effort and attention required to achieve success.

He also connected with people through golf. A good player who could handle pressure, Fr. Riehle performed in the clutch. Anyone who could not resist making a small wager on a golf game or a particular putt with Fr. Riehle learned that such bravado may result in a lesson in humility and a wallet a couple of bucks lighter.

Fr. Riehle tried to aid everyone in doing their best. As a result, a stream of people would come to Fr. Riehle's office to see him each Friday before a home football game to share stories, thank him for his guidance and enjoy some laughs. Many of them would not have attained the success they ultimately achieved without Fr. Riehle and they wanted to let him know they appreciated him making such a positive difference in their lives.

This book is filled with priceless stories. If you want to be inspired to become the best person you can be, read this book. If you want to help your spouse, daughters, sons, nieces, nephews, other family members and friends to show resolve in the face of adversity, give them this book. If you seek to preserve the proven lessons for living that helped high-profile people attain success and keep their priorities in proper perspective, you'll appreciate this book. Fr. Riehle had a gift for listening to people, hearing about their hopes and helping them to fulfill their dreams. The timeless advice that he gave and the selfless way that he tried to live are worth preserving and sharing. Trust me; the golden guidance offered by this championship chaplain not only can benefit us but help future generations, too.

INTRODUCTION

He never threw a touchdown pass, scored a game-winning goal or called a play to set up a buzzer-beating basket to turn a would-be loss into a triumph for the University of Notre Dame but Fr. James Riehle may have been just as important to the school as anyone who ever achieved those feats. Fr. Riehle had a unique role of serving as a confidant, adviser and motivational force to those who attained high levels of success, as well as endured the criticism that can accompany public failure. People naturally face emotional ups and downs in life but Fr. Riehle was the go-to person for many individuals who needed to rebound from defeats, both large and small. Those who sought his guidance include some of the most adulated athletes and coaches in America who shared his connection to Notre Dame.

Fr. Riehle worked as a salesman before becoming a priest and gained unique insights into human nature that allowed him to discern when a person needed a pat on the back or a verbal kick in the pants. His work experience before he became a priest helped him develop his gift for connecting with people of various backgrounds and religious beliefs to propel them to pursue their potential. He could be tough, compassionate and motivating in the same conversation. He would listen to someone, assess the situation and then make a sincere attempt to direct that person along the path that he felt the individual needed to take. People may not have always liked what Fr. Riehle said or the blunt way he sometimes expressed it, but he gained a well-earned reputation as the kind of man who would tell others what he thought they needed to know rather than what they wanted to hear. If a person was ready for an honest reality check, Fr. Riehle could be counted on to give it.

The value of his counsel proved instrumental in aiding many people in overcoming their difficulties. Even though those who benefitted from his guidance largely came from the Notre Dame community, the direction he provided to those who sought him out transcends the scope of his service at a single university. Frankly, Notre Dame is both loved and reviled in a world of people who may be attracted to a religious institution named to honor Christ's mother or repelled by it. But if religious biases and athletic rivalries are set aside, people who live and work beyond Notre Dame can learn from the life of Fr. Riehle, who led people through turbulent times and played a behind-the-scenes role in their ultimate success.

Without realizing it, many readers already may be familiar with Fr. Riehle. Anyone who ever watched the movie *Rudy* has seen Fr. Riehle in action. Fr. Riehle appeared as the priest who recited the "Hail Mary" in the pivotal locker room scene before the walk-on player nicknamed "Rudy" took the field in his only game as a Notre Dame football player. The scene showed Fr. Riehle in his role as a dependable spiritual leader for the players, coaches and support staffers who turned to him during times of extreme struggle and stress.

Fr. Riehle also appeared in a television commercial with Joe Montana, a great Notre Dame quarterback and four-time Super Bowl champ with the San Francisco 49ers. The commercial for Adidas featured Montana returning to campus for a visit and receiving a warm greeting from Fr. Riehle. The pair displayed a comfortable rapport as they walked and talked. The scene ended with Fr. Riehle supplying the punch line for a humorous conclusion, as the priest liked to do as he performed his duties as the school's sports chaplain.

Despite his often serious demeanor, Fr. Riehle also displayed a sense of humor that athletes, in particular, appreciated to ease stress as the time neared for a game to begin. He enjoyed a good laugh as much as anyone and seemed to relish such moments, even when he was the target of someone else's joke. His tough-guy exterior helped to make the priest's quick-witted quips even funnier. When tension mounted and the nerves of those around him began to fray, Fr. Riehle could use humor to lighten the mood.

Some of the university's most accomplished student-athletes, coaches, professors, administrators and others consider Fr. Riehle as much of a Notre Dame institution during his decades of service there as the "Golden Dome" of the Main Building, the Grotto of Our Lady of Lourdes and the "Touchdown Jesus" mural on the facade of the 14-story Hesburgh Library. Fr. Riehle was a spiritual guide to so many people that his advice for living, and especially how to overcome adversity, became worthy of chronicling and preserving.

Each of the eight chapters in this book focuses on a different way to enhance the quality and the purpose of life. Fr. Riehle endured a number of personal hardships, so he knew first hand that a crisis can occur at any time. He also understood that life is relatively short and frequently deviates from our plans, so a resilient spirit is important to develop and to put into practice. In his final years, Fr. Riehle lost both of his legs to diabetes but he showed how to endure physical infirmities with stoic strength and to find fulfillment by helping others.

Fr. Riehle was a man others wanted on their side when life's pressures and disappointments hit them as hard as a blitzing linebacker. Many people interviewed for this book described how the priest's concern and counsel steered them away from dejection, frustration and needless anxiety. The following pages offer directions for life that tap the timeless wisdom that Fr. Riehle shared with the people around him. If he still were alive today to talk to us, it seems safe to conclude that his hope would be that his life and the lessons that he shared with those he guided will leave readers inspired and focused on seizing the opportunities that each new day brings.

Chapter 1

BUILD A FOUNDATION

The defining moment in Fr. James Riehle's life may have occurred during his freshman year at the University of Notre Dame when he learned that his father had died unexpectedly of a heart attack. The need to face a family crisis and put the interests of others before his own in that situation aided him later in helping those who sought his guidance in tackling their own challenges. He excelled in life as an adviser, especially for those under heightened stress.

His experience of overcoming the untimely loss of a father also helped him to understand that how a person responds to misfortune is a critical factor in whether a situation worsens or allows emotional healing to begin. Compassion, generosity and kindness from others can help to ease a difficult time. Lessons learned from coping with the loss of his father endured and had a transformative effect on the young James Riehle. That crisis also may have helped to prepare him for later when he became a priest who provided fatherly advice (and often tough love) to Notre Dame students, including star athletes.

Oscar Wilde wrote, "What fire does not destroy, it hardens." Fr. Riehle became living proof of that view of life as he faced various hardships and disappointments that might have caused others to unravel but left him with a steely resolve to accept his proverbial crosses and persevere.

Dad's Death

The responsibility of informing James Riehle of his father's death on January 12, 1946, fell to a young priest, Fr. Theodore Hesburgh, who served as the rector of the Badin Hall dormitory where Riehle lived. His father, just 56 years old, had come home from work and was dead "three hours later," Joan Riehle Ruse, Fr. Riehle's sister recounted.

Years later, Fr. Hesburgh became the university's visionary president who led the school to international prominence, while the student who lost his father that cold winter day ultimately discerned a call to the priesthood and developed into a valued administrator and fellow clergyman at Notre Dame.

On the day of his dad's death, James Riehle faced the dual realities of trying to fathom the magnitude of his loss and of finding a way home for the funeral in Pittsburgh. With the death of his family's breadwinner, the student turned elsewhere to pay for his bus fare home from Notre Dame's campus in South Bend, Indiana.

Generous Gentlemen

As word spread about his plight, priests and fellow students at Badin Hall quickly pooled together their meager funds to send Jim Riehle on his way. None of them probably could have envisioned that the student ultimately would return the kindness by becoming a key fundraiser for student scholarships when he returned to Notre Dame later to serve as a priest. It seems that the personal hardship that he endured with the death of his dad galvanized his resolve to assist others in need.

Part of that motivation likely stemmed from the abrupt interruption of his studies. Without the money to stay at Notre Dame, James Riehle moved back home to his family in Pittsburgh and began taking courses at Duquesne University. But his return home also allowed him to bond with his much-younger sister Joan.

James drove Joan to and from her job each day. Those car rides gave them a chance to talk and get to know each other better. They forged a bond on those commutes that bridged the seven-year age difference that limited their friendship during their childhood.

Modest Man

"My brother didn't talk about himself," Joan said. "It was like pulling teeth to find out what was going on with him."

Even though Fr. Riehle was reticent to discuss himself, he became a favorite of others who chose to share their worries with him.

His advice typically proved to be insightful, even if what he said was not what a person desired to hear from him. His straightforwardness, however, earned the respect of others, who learned that they could count on the sometimes gruff clergyman to tell them the unadorned truth.

Decades of Service

Fr. Riehle served the university faithfully in one capacity or another for all or parts of five decades from the turbulent days of student rebellion in the 1960s to the early 2000s. He left a lasting impression on many, from the most lauded engineering professors to the biggest and toughest football players.

Gerry Faust, Notre Dame's head football coach from 1981 to 1985, said he will never forget Fr. Riehle's devotion in blessing each player, one-by-one, as the team returned to the locker room following pre-game warm-ups and again as they each re-entered the locker room at the conclusion of a game.

"Each player would kneel down in front of him and Fr. Jim would give him a blessing," Faust recalled. Fr. Riehle would put a hand on the player's shoulder or head and give a blessing with his other hand.

Whether the results on the field matched the dreams of an individual player or coach varied, but Fr. Riehle provided a spiritual presence and a listening ear if the participants later turned to him for solace.

Lifelong Sportsman

Fr. Riehle loved sports and especially enjoyed watching ESPN to see games and highlights in his final years after health problems left him with minimal mobility. Diabetes unfortunately led to the amputation of both of his feet. A stroke in 2004 hurt his memory. But he still could offer blessings and spiritual guidance.

One of Fr. Riehle's greatest contributions to the Notre Dame football team took the form of pep talks that he mixed into the homily of each pre-game Mass. The priest spoke in a way that connected with the players.

"He had a unique gift," Faust recalled.

The chaplain's "down to Earth" approach allowed him to communicate in a manner that let everyone understand his messages, Faust said. After his pre-game sermon, every player was fired up and ready to go out and take the field.

"Fr. Jim gave better pep talks than I did before the game," Faust said humbly. "He fit his pep talks into his homilies. I've been around a lot of priests and our football team chaplain gave the greatest pep talks."

Montana's Motivational Maestro

"I think he [Fr. Jim Riehle] was just one of those special guys who had a long association with the university and touched a lot of people's lives," said Joe Montana, a former Notre Dame quarterback who led the team to a national championship during 1977. "A lot of people were thankful that he was around."

The priest's sense of humor was exemplified when he appeared in a television commercial with Montana. The funniest moment belonged to Fr. Riehle. When asked by this author what he thought about someone from the clergy delivering the punch line, Montana good naturedly said, "Don't they always?"

Montana showed up to tape the television commercial on the Notre Dame campus without knowing that the role of the priest would be played by the team's chaplain.

"It was nice that they picked him," Montana said. "They made it a lot more comfortable, since I knew him so well many years ago."

Fit to Be Tied

Fr. Riehle had a "big influence" on the football team, said Ara Parseghian, who worked alongside the priest from 1966 until the coach's retirement in 1974.

"I spent a lot of time with him," Parseghian said. "Our relationship became close in 1966, when he was first assigned as the chaplain to the football team. Of course, that was in the latter part of the season. Our previous chaplain had passed away."

Fr. Riehle's first game as the team chaplain finished in a historic, 10-10 tie in 1966 that pitted second-ranked Michigan State against top-ranked Notre Dame.

Parseghian recalled receiving "a lot of static" for tying the Spartans. A number of critics claimed Parseghian should have been more aggressive in his play calling late in the game to win the contest rather than settle for a tie. However, Parseghian said his team played too hard and too well amid injuries to key players for him to take unreasonable risks that might cause the game to be lost in the final minutes. By virtue of not losing to second-ranked Michigan State, however, Notre Dame won the national championship that season.

As the years passed and the personal relationship between the pair strengthened, Parseghian began to joke with Fr. Riehle that the blame for Notre Dame tying rather than beating the Spartans that day belonged to the team's then-rookie chaplain.

"As time moved forward, I kept saying, 'I guess that was your fault, Father, not mine. You were the chaplain of that team.' We used to kid about that from the time of 1966 all the way up until the time that he passed away," Parseghian said.

Ironically, even though many people, including certain coaches, thought having a chaplain on the sideline might provide an edge in a close game, Fr. Riehle was not one who would pray for divine intervention to win. But the chaplain built a strong foundation with his pre-game Masses that motivated the players and the coaches.

Mentoring Moments for 'RUDY'

Dreams give people hope to help them to forge ahead when they encounter life's pitfalls. Fr. Riehle's role sometimes was as simple as urging someone not to become defeatist when a chance for redemption was on the horizon. Fr. Riehle encouraged people to rebound from disappointments in a positive way through hard work, tenacity and an unrelenting sense of hope.

Such conversations turned into "mentoring moments," recalled backup Notre Dame football player Dan "Rudy" Ruettiger. He was a walk-on player during the 1970s and gained acclaim as a consummate underdog on the athletic field and in life during the 1993 movie about him fulfilling his long-shot dream of attending the university and earning a spot on its storied football team.

Fr. Riehle and other several priests at Notre Dame were portrayed in the film through a single character called Fr. Cavanaugh. The movie's time limitations did not allow every influential person in his life to be included individually, Rudy conceded.

"In the movie, it was impossible to take all of the characters who were in my life at Notre Dame and re-make them, so we did a lot of composites in the characters to make them one," Rudy said.

However, Fr. Riehle himself prayed the "Hail Mary" in the movie before the only game in which the walk-on athlete played. The prayer reflects devotion to the university's namesake, "Our Lady," the mother of Christ. In a display of reverence, all of the players on the team went to their knees when Fr. Riehle recited the prayer. The scene in the locker room before the game could not have been much more authentic, since Fr. Riehle had led Notre Dame players in that prayer for decades.

No-Nonsense Nudging

When Rudy was emotionally worn down from bruising football practices, Fr. Riehle served as an unofficial life coach. Fr. Riehle reminded Rudy that he was fulfilling a dream at Notre Dame. The priest would explain that the Notre Dame experience was about more than pursuing ambitions on the football field and that Rudy should be thankful for the opportunity to show that he belonged there.

Fr. Riehle openly acknowledged that victories in football are great to accomplish and to celebrate, especially since they boost the university's image and give hope to people who admire and vicariously identify with the school, Rudy said. Fr. Riehle also emphasized the importance of a person persevering not only in football and in school but in life.

Fr. Riehle shared that message consistently with student-athletes at Notre Dame, regardless of whether someone was a backup player such as Rudy or a star athlete.

"You can't quit because things aren't going your way," Rudy said he remembered Fr. Riehle telling him. "You can't quit because things don't seem to be what you thought they should be. You're at Notre Dame. This is it. This is Notre Dame. Don't quit on something that you believe in and that you have faith in."

At times, Rudy needed to be reminded that he was fulfilling his fantasy, despite the frustrations.

"When I walked on campus, it was more of a cleansing of getting rid of all of the nonsense and all of the doubt that I had in myself, after people told me for years and years and years that I cannot go to Notre Dame," Rudy said. "'You don't belong here at Notre Dame. You don't have the grades to be at Notre Dame.'"

Fr. Riehle counterbalanced the critics by advising that a student belonged at Notre Dame, "if you put forth the effort," Rudy said. The priest stressed the need to pursue worthwhile personal and spiritual goals.

Rudy created a favorable public image for both Notre Dame and Ruettiger. As an author and motivational speaker, Rudy effectively has turned his unquenchable desire to lift the human spirit into his life's work. He now advises others, just as Fr. Riehle urged him, to go after their dreams and soul-stirring activities.

Inclusive Chaplain

Notre Dame had players of varying religious beliefs, so Fr. Riehle said he tried to focus his homilies during each pre-game Mass on the football game that would follow. The players seemed to respond to the priest's inspiring words. Even non-Catholic players complimented the priest's homilies.

Raghib "Rocket" Ismail, a wide receiver from Wilkes-Barre, Pennsylvania, may have been among the best kickoff return men in the history of college football. He stood next to Fr. Riehle one day in a campus gym and said that he was really looking forward to the upcoming football season. When Fr. Riehle asked why, Ismail said it was because he enjoyed attending the pre-game Masses so much.

The comment was all the more remarkable because Ismail's family had introduced him to the Muslim faith during his childhood.

Reggie Brooks, a former Notre Dame running back, was among the many non-Catholic players on the team during his college years, but he liked the religion's focus on serving others. Brooks said he, too, particularly looked forward to the pre-game Masses celebrated by Fr. Riehle. In addition, Brooks said he admired Fr. Riehle's compassion, a trait that shone through in the Masses, in blessings just before players left the locker room to begin games, in brief conversations and in many other ways.

"He truly cared," Brooks said. Despite his rugged persona, Fr. Riehle could put high-energy football players who might be overly anxious at ease about whatever would transpire on a given day, Brooks added.

Before his playing days ended, Brooks rushed for 1,063 yards during his rookie season with the Washington Redskins. Injuries shortened his career but he later returned to Notre Dame to work as an administrator in the athletic department. In fact, Brooks works with the Monogram Club, a lettermen's organization that Fr. Riehle once led as its executive director during a time when it expanded its scholarship program significantly to help the sons and daughters of former athletes attend the school.

Methodist Mass Attendee

"I was a Methodist, but yet I never missed a Mass," said Joe Theismann, a former Notre Dame quarterback who later played the same position in leading the Washington Redskins to a Super Bowl championship. "When you saw [Fr. Riehle], you just felt better."

One of Theismann's favorite places of refuge in college, even though he was not especially religious, was attending Fr. Riehle's Masses.

"It was funny," Theismann said. "My dad was Catholic but we grew up worshipping in the Methodist church."

Theismann was raised in the pre-Vatican II era, when the Catholic Mass used Latin rather than the native language of the attendees. Despite the language barrier, he appreciated the tradition and the ritual of the Catholic religious services.

It was "calming" to alternate between kneeling and sitting, while listening to the Mass in Latin, Theismann said.

Rockne-Like Rock

When asked to describe Fr. Riehle, Theismann conjured up images of famed Notre Dame Coach Knute Rockne by saying, "The man was a rock. Water beats against it. Wind beats against it. You can chip away at it. But it's still as solid as can be. And that's what he became, I think, for so many of us that really went through life changes at that age."

Scholarship football players typically arrive on campus after having been high school stars but that acclaim is inadequate preparation for the attention that accompanies high-profile athletes at Notre Dame, Theismann said. In the 1960s, students had plenty of potential distractions that included protests, parties and other extracurricular activities. Despite limited time, Notre Dame student-athletes faced high expectations. They also had a chaplain who, for many of them, assumed the role of a surrogate father when they needed one.

Father Figure

"The term, Father, I think, fit him so well because he truly was a father figure," Theismann said. Other ways exist to refer to "men of the cloth," but none of them fit Fr. Riehle quite as well, Theismann said.

"He was a father for so many of us," Theismann said. "Remember, we're 17- and 18-year-old kids. This is our first time away from home. You're basically on your own. You think you're a man and you think that you've got life handled and you think you can handle every situation. But the truth of the matter is you can't.

"He was that calming force, that father figure, who you could always turn to in a time of need. I never really had the occasion to sit down and have a heart-to-heart with him. But I felt like if I ever needed to go somewhere, he was No. 1 on my list."

Fr. Riehle's presence around the team seemed to sway the players to behave more responsibly than typically might be expected of a college student, Theismann said.

"You sort of felt like your dad was watching," Theismann said. "You really couldn't cut lose and go totally crazy because Father would know. He best fits that title of the old television show, 'Father Knows Best.' He did [know best]."

The priest had a "great presence on the campus," Theismann said. For example, Fr. Riehle had a "very distinctive gait" that allowed an onlooker to recognize him walking from a distance, Theismann added.

At times, Fr. Riehle could be "very stern," much the way that a father might react when he needed to correct the wayward conduct of a misbehaving son, said Theismann, who attended Notre Dame at a time when only men were admitted as students.

"There was always this calming effect that he had on us," Theismann said. "I know that we were lucky enough not to lose many football games, but if we did, he hurt as badly as we did."

Fr. Riehle served as a spiritual sentinel for students, despite his tough-looking exterior.

"He'd always have a cigar hanging out of his mouth," Theismann recalled. Fr. Riehle's competitive spirit also distinguished him from other priests who might appear and act more traditionally pious.

"I guess when you grow up and have this vision of a priest, the vision doesn't fit cigar smoking and golf playing," Theismann said. "Times are different now, but I don't think back then that's the vision that people had. He was a priest but I'd also describe him as a man's man."

The characteristics of a rugged former soldier, a competitor and a faithful clergyman made Fr. Riehle an ideal chaplain for an athletic team, Theismann said.

Hoops Homilist

Fr. Riehle not only served as the head sports chaplain for several decades starting in 1973 but he also traveled with the basketball team for a number of games and tournaments himself. If he could not attend a game for any reason, he arranged for another priest to wear a religious collar and to sit courtside with the Notre Dame basketball team to show the university's Catholic identity.

"He was a very good motivator," said Richard "Digger" Phelps, a former Notre Dame basketball coach who later became an ESPN sports analyst. "His homilies were excellent."

Fr. Riehle always would inspire the players by using the readings at the Mass, regardless of the sport.

Phelps joked that he would caution Fr. Riehle to keep his game-day Mass to no more than 20 minutes, since the pre-game meal would follow immediately thereafter. Fr. Riehle's campus-wide reputation for giving quick Masses made him a natural to fulfill that request.

"We never prayed to win," Phelps said. "We always prayed to do our best."

Chapter 2

STRENGTHEN YOUR SUPPORT SYSTEM

Born Near Boston

Fr. Riehle's entrance into the world came in sports-loving New England. The oldest of three children, James Riehle was born on November 25, 1924, in Medford, Massachusetts, a suburb of his mother's home town of Everett, Massachusetts, just outside of Boston. Fr. Riehle's mother, whose maiden name was Matilda Kathryn McAfee, married his father, Louis Clemens Riehle, a native of Perintown, Ohio. The priest's mother manifested her appreciation of a strong support system, as well as love for her family and her native New England, by returning from Ohio to Massachusetts for the birth of her first child, James, and his brother, Al, two years later.

"My mother didn't feel anybody out West knew how to deliver her babies," her daughter and youngest child, Joan Riehle Ruse said.

Flint's Finest

The lure of aunts and other relatives who lived in Massachusetts waned by the time Joan was due to be delivered when the family had moved from Columbus, Ohio, to Flint, Michigan. Mrs. Riehle apparently was impressed enough with the doctors in Flint to give birth to her only daughter there in 1931.

They also had two step-sisters, Frances and Lorena, from Louis Riehle's marriage to his first wife, Gertrude, who shockingly died of meningitis at the age of 23 while her husband was in France fighting a war. With a father overseas serving in the military, the two girls essentially became orphans for a while, so they ended up living with one of Fr. Riehle's 11 uncles until their father's return. Louis Riehle later married Matilda and they raised all five children together under the same roof.

When baby Joan was about 18 months old, the family moved to Saginaw, Michigan, about 40 miles north of Flint along I-75, where Louis took a job with Shelby SalesBook Co. Jim later would work for the same company for several years in Detroit before he became a priest.

Spirit of Saginaw

The Riehle family enjoyed sports year-round and would turn their back-yard in Saginaw every winter into a skating rink.

"So, we all skated from the time we could walk," Joan said. "That is probably where Jim started his hockey, in the backyard."

He would later become the captain of his high school hockey team, and he never lost his enthusiasm for the sport. In fact, he usually chose to travel with the Notre Dame hockey team to games as its chaplain when he had the option to go himself.

Along with his life-long love of sports, James also showed a devotion to the Lord at a tender age.

Boyhood Dream

Fr. Riehle's interest in becoming a priest began early in his childhood.

"Jim wanted to be a priest from the time he was a little boy," Joan said. "In fact, we used to play Mass. Jim would always be the priest. My brother Al was always the altar boy and I, of course, always was the congregation."

For Communion hosts, the children used Necco wafers, a classic American candy sold in rolls. Each wafer featured one of eight pastel colors and a corresponding flavor—chocolate, lemon, lime, orange, clove, wintergreen, cinnamon and licorice. Most clergymen would love to have a congregation as dedicated to attending services as Joan. Her avid attendance, however, could at least partially be attributed to the candy wafers.

"I loved to play it because I got the Necco wafers," Joan said. "I can remember it as if it was yesterday. And I was very little when I started to play that."

"Joan loved chocolate Necco wafers her whole life," said her daughter-in-law Jeannine Ruse. "Whenever I could find a roll of chocolate, I always bought them for her. I'm sure it brought back a lot of childhood memories for her."

Credit her brother James for promoting both Joan's love for Necco wafers *and* the Eucharist while she was a little girl.

In fact, James played the role of a priest during his childhood "almost constantly," Joan recalled. When he finished eighth grade and entered high school, he aspired to join a minor seminary to begin his path toward the priesthood.

"My father wouldn't let him because he thought he was too young to make the decision," Joan said. Instead, James and his brother Al both attended and graduated from St. Andrew's High School in Saginaw. Joan attended St. Andrew's Grade School before the family moved to Pittsburgh in 1943 when their father accepted a job transfer to become a sales manager.

Emphasized Education

Anyone who may have wondered why Fr. Riehle became such a strong advocate for the pursuit of education need look no further than his own determination not to let his father's death stop him from continuing his studies. He ultimately received a Bachelor of Science degree in 1949 from Notre Dame and Bachelor of Business degree from Duquesne University in 1950.

The discipline he obtained from his Catholic upbringing, followed by his 1950-52 service in the U.S. Army, also shaped Fr. Riehle. Many people who knew him well remarked about their respect for Fr. Riehle as a man who could lead and help to mold students to fulfill their potential. Naturally, as a one-time military man, Fr. Riehle could both give and follow orders. Nonetheless, the former salesman was adept at waiting patiently for people to approach him about spiritual questions and then trying to guide them as part of their support system.

After serving in the U.S. Army and later working successfully as a salesman, Jim Riehle ultimately discerned that he should become a man of the cloth. He entered the Sacred Heart Novitiate in Jordan, Minnesota, and made his first vows on his path to priesthood there on August 16, 1958.

To further his formation to become a priest, he studied at Holy Cross College in Washington, D.C., between 1960 and 1964. His ordination as a deacon occurred in 1963 at the Shrine of the Immaculate Conception in Washington, D.C. Fr. Riehle's ordination as a priest at age 39 occurred on June 10, 1964, at the Basilica of the Sacred Heart at Notre Dame. He celebrated his first Mass as a priest at St. Thomas More Catholic Church in Troy, Michigan. By then, Fr. Riehle's mother had remarried and moved to the neighboring Detroit suburb of Birmingham.

Fr. Riehle became chaplain at Dillon Hall on Notre Dame's campus during his first assignment as a priest. He then went to Sacred Heart Parish in New Orleans but returned to Notre Dame in 1966 to serve as the university's assistant dean of students and as rector of Sorin Hall. He assumed the critical role of dean of students—the chief disciplinarian of students at the university—in 1967 and held that post until after the end of the Vietnam War in 1973. For 12 years, until 1985, he served as rector of Pangborn Hall. Other key roles Fr. Riehle filled at Notre Dame included chairing the board of directors for the University Club, 1971-77, and directing energy conservation, 1973-93.

As a priest, Fr. Riehle capped off his pursuit of higher education by earning a Master's of Science degree in business administration from Notre

Dame in 1978. He used that training effectively as executive director of the university's Monogram Club between 1978 and 2002 in boosting its coffers to become a key source of scholarships at the school for the children of former Notre Dame athletes.

However, Fr. Riehle's favorite role was athletic chaplain. Even though his first game as a football chaplain took place in 1966, he did not officially become the athletic department's head chaplain until 1973. But even before then he became a valued and trusted guide to coaches and players who knew firsthand the cauldron-like heat that is felt by people in prominent positions who face enormous expectations.

Canadian Vacation

Coach Faust described Fr. Riehle as a loyal and trustworthy friend. Faust remembers when his family took a vacation in Canada during his tenure as Notre Dame's head football coach and invited Fr. Riehle to join them. The team chaplain became a family favorite.

"We went out fishing each morning," Faust said. "Things weren't going really well for me, as far as wins and losses. We ate after Mass and took a break to play cards."

Faust said his kids still talk about how much they all enjoyed the trip. The priest was "very open" about whatever he was thinking, Faust added. Despite only meeting Fr. Riehle after arriving at Notre Dame, Faust said they formed a deep bond.

"He was like a brother to me," Faust said. "He was not afraid to tell you how he sees a situation. He loved being a priest."

Visiting the Garden

Coach Phelps and Fr. Riehle especially enjoyed visiting New York City when the basketball team played at Madison Square Garden. After the game, they headed with a small entourage to P.J. Clarke's, a restaurant known for turning cheeseburgers into delicacies. While there, Fr. Riehle displayed his characteristic frankness by second guessing any of Phelps' decisions during the game that the chaplain felt he needed to bring up.

"Why'd you make that move, Digger?" Phelps recalled Fr. Riehle asking. "He was just a classic in that."

Fr. Riehle's directness may be the one quality above all others that made him "such a great priest," Phelps said.

"He was honest and open and would not go behind your back," Phelps said. "If there were issues, he would talk about them."

Bench Buddy

One of Notre Dame's most devoted basketball fans was Ed O'Rourke, a retired Chicago attorney who sat at the end of the team bench with Fr. Riehle for 100-plus games. O'Rourke graduated from Notre Dame in 1949 with a double major in political science and philosophy. He never married, so he took advantage of the flexibility in his personal life to attend more than 95 percent of the team's basketball games, both home and away, starting in 1956. Only funerals, weddings and other rare occasions prevented him from attending every game before he died in June 2012. O'Rourke estimated that he watched Notre Dame's basketball team play more than 1,300 games.

"I don't miss many," O'Rourke said. He also tried to attend all of the Notre Dame home football games. However, he expressed a preference for traveling to the basketball games, since it is a "far more intimate" atmosphere than joining the throngs of fans who take road trips to watch Fighting Irish football. O'Rourke's dedication in backing Notre Dame led him to form a friendship and a support system with Fr. Riehle that strengthened as they sat on the team bench together year-after-year at basketball games.

Loved Hockey

Despite Fr. Riehle's bond to the basketball team, hockey proved to be his "No. 1" love, Phelps said. "He was always traveling with the hockey team."

Fr. Riehle's participation as a roughhousing player in the lunchtime faculty and staff hockey games on campus became widely known. The priest played the game the way he learned it during his teen-age years in Michigan.

O'Rourke, on the other hand, played high school basketball and he really appreciated the nuances of the game in a way that many others could not. It is not unlike a trained artist recognizing the consummate skill of a master. That background gave O'Rourke credibility in explaining that Fr. Riehle limited voicing his displeasure at games to occasions when basketball officials actually made "bad calls" against Notre Dame. The officials themselves might take a different view but none of them ever became so incensed with the priest's commentary to penalize the Notre Dame team for it.

Technical Foul?

One night at Madison Square Garden in New York, Fr. Riehle sat near the end of the Notre Dame basketball team's bench next to super-fan O'Rourke for a key game with about 16,000 people in attendance. Fr. Riehle objected to questionable calls during the game and he voiced his displeasure audibly to the officials.

The referee walked over to Phelps to tell him that if the priest did not "lay off" about criticizing the officiating, the padre's comments would draw a technical foul for the team. Phelps then went to the end of the bench to warn the chaplain.

"I said, 'Fr. Jim, I understand that you and the official have an issue.' He looks at me, starts staring at me and then turns to look at Eddie. I said, 'no, no, no, don't look at Eddie. I'm looking at you. He [the official] said 'priest.' Please don't get me a technical."

Fr. Riehle quelled voicing his opinion about the officiating as the game continued and Notre Dame ultimately won. Phelps said he could not remember the opponent but he retained a vivid recollection of the curmudgeonly chaplain's willingness to express himself openly and honestly at courtside.

"That was pretty classic—where he almost gets a technical for screaming at the referee about a bad call," Phelps said.

A spirited supporter of Notre Dame, Fr. Riehle needed to learn to pick his spots about what to say to the officials, how to phrase it and when to speak.

"He would not be afraid to bark at a call," Phelps said about Fr. Riehle.

In the end, Fr. Riehle finished his career as the team chaplain without ever drawing a technical foul for Notre Dame.

"I'm the only one who ever got a technical," Phelps quipped.

Chaplain's Chum

Outside of Phelps' ear shot, Fr. Riehle's exact interaction with the referee was unknown to the coach but not to O'Rourke, who defended the priest's behavior.

"He [Fr. Riehle] wasn't way out of line or anything," O'Rourke said. "Referees have a way of making mistakes. Some referees seem to have rabbit ears and hear everything. Fr. Riehle probably just said, 'You blew that one.'"

Of course, Fr. Riehle's authoritative way of expressing himself as a man of deep conviction likely irritated the referee, who warned the coach to "calm the Reverend," O'Rourke recalled.

Dining on Delicacies

Basketball also facilitated the friendship between O'Rourke and Fr. Riehle, since far fewer people trek to watch games on the road than in football and the travel arrangements are much easier.

"Fr. Riehle loved dining and going to the best restaurants in whatever city that he was visiting," O'Rourke said.

The priest, in particular, appreciated good food, especially if the price was right, O'Rourke said. If Fr. Riehle received an invitation to dinner, he'd sometimes inquire where his prospective host planned to take him, his friend said.

Fr. Riehle often had more than one offer to join people for dinner. People who think that the life of a clergyman who takes vows of poverty and celibacy would be an ascetic and lonely existence likely never had seen Fr. Riehle and his wide network of friends, acquaintances and the Notre Dame graduates who treated him to meals, games of golf and first-rate cigars.

The chaplain's sister Joan and the rest of his family kidded him about eating meals at white-tablecloth restaurants, playing golf at elite private courses and enjoying other such invitations more frequently than anyone else they knew.

"I said to him, 'I wish I had taken a vow of poverty like you took,'" Joan said. "I told him that all the time and he'd just roll his eyes."

Engineering a Friendship

Al Szewczyk, a Notre Dame professor who also served about 10 years as chairman of the university's aerospace and mechanical engineering department during the 1980s, regarded Fr. Riehle as a close friend, even though the chaplain would bump him around during faculty hockey games. Not only did they meet regularly for lunch as part of the unofficial campus group known as the Algonquin Table, the priest also was an occasional dinner guest at the professor's home.

"We really became friends when he was the dean of students," Szewczyk said. The priest, of course, had the unenviable task of persuading students one way or another to obey Fr. Hesburgh's rule to cease and desist any protests within 15 minutes, if university officials concluded that the activities disrupted other students from obtaining their educations.

When he served as the university's top disciplinarian during the 1960s, Fr. Riehle's photo appeared in the *Observer*, a Notre Dame student newspaper. The Szewczyk family cut out the photo and put it on their home's front door in anticipation of the priest's arrival for dinner that evening. Underneath the photo, they wrote the words, "Our Hero," Szewczyk recalled.

"He appreciated that very much," Szewczyk said. Upon setting foot in the house, Fr. Riehle, knowing he now was in friendly territory and could relax, said he needed a martini, Szewczyk recalled. The priest's remark drew laughter from his hosts. His quips seemed particularly amusing when he eschewed political correctness. In such instances, his direct style of speaking often omitted the kinds of diplomatic words that one might expect to hear from a clergyman.

Golfing Buddy

Fr. Riehle exhibited immense passion for sports. He showed his competitiveness as an avid and accomplished golfer, as well as when he served as captain of his high school hockey team in Saginaw, Michigan.

The genuineness of Fr. Riehle's personality helped to make him a popular golfing buddy for Szewczyk and many others. Fr. Riehle's love of golf was widely known among former Notre Dame athletes and students who occasionally provided him with gifts that added to his array of golf clubs. Anyone wanting to buy something for Fr. Riehle knew that he would be an appreciative recipient of golf equipment.

"I always used to laugh when he opened up the trunk of his car," said Marty Allen, a former football team manager and Monogram Club board member. "It looked like the inside of a pro shop at a golf course. He had more golf equipment in the back than I've ever seen in my life."

"He really had a good golf game, excellent putter and chipper, etc.," said Lou Holtz, a College Football Hall of Fame inductee who was Notre Dame's head coach between 1986 and 1996.

Holtz enjoyed many hours on the golf course with Fr. Riehle. The time away from the football field may have been therapeutic.

"We had so much fun," Holtz said. "We played a lot of golf together."

A frequent foursome featured former Notre Dame men's and women's golf coach George Thomas, Fr. Riehle, retired Notre Dame football coach Ara Parseghian and Holtz. They competed but shared laughs, too.

"I'll never forget that Ara and I lost $5 or something like that to Fr. Riehle," Holtz recalled. "Ara said to Fr. Riehle, 'I'll put it in the collection basket for you.'"

Inter-Denominational Debt

Parseghian, a non-Catholic, would have been putting the money into the collection plate at the church of a different religious denomination. The occasion occurred at a golf fundraiser for Notre Dame's Monogram Club.

"Father was a pretty good golfer," Parseghian said. "He could have hot and cold rounds."

Fr. Riehle played so well the day of the bet that Parseghian said he began to do everything he could to distract the priest. Nothing seemed to cool off the clergyman's sizzling round of golf.

"I rattled coins," Parseghian said. "I talked to him. I gave him all the needle I could to try to un-track him from his golf game. Well, he continued right on as if absolutely nothing bothered him."

California, Here He Comes

After Holtz led Notre Dame to the 1988 national football title in Phoenix with a 34 to 21 victory against West Virginia University in the Fiesta Bowl, Fr. Riehle traveled to California after he arranged to use a home in Monterrey to play golf at Pebble Beach. O'Rourke joined him and they tried to obtain tee times to play the course once they arrived.

A worker at the golf course said it was closed to the public due to the Bing Crosby golf tournament. However, people who stayed at the lodge still could play on the course during certain times.

Fr. Riehle and O'Rourke were looking at shirts in the pro shop when the head golf professional appeared and began talking to Fr. Riehle and his guest about the national championship football game. When Fr. Riehle mentioned that he had been there and was the Notre Dame football team chaplain, they only talked a little while longer before the golf pro said that he thought he could arrange for the visitors to play the next day, O'Rourke said.

When the assistant started to make the arrangements, he told Fr. Riehle and his guest that they would need to pay a higher price to play golf, since they were not staying at the lodge. Suddenly, it became clear that the golf pro, who had re-entered his office nearby, was listening to the conversation.

"They are staying at the lodge," the golf pro told his colleague.

It marked another example of why Fr. Riehle developed the nickname "America's guest." Wherever he went, hospitality seemed to come his way.

Wherever Fr. Riehle would go, he usually knew someone who belonged to a country club where a game of golf could be arranged, said Marty Gleason, a former president the Notre Dame Club of Chicago.

Racquet Ball Quartet

The chaplain's support system extended well beyond his golf buddies. Fr. Riehle, one-time head athletic trainer John Whitmer, the university's first varsity hockey coach Charles "Lefty" Smith and former Notre Dame Sports Information Director Roger Valdiserri competed regularly in racquet ball. Whitmer and Smith typically teamed up against Fr. Riehle and Valdiserri.

"Lefty was no shrinking violet and I'm bigger than Lefty," Whitmer said. "Lefty and I could provide quite an obstacle in doubles."

Fr. Riehle displayed his competitive nature by occasionally hitting the ball off the back or the leg of an opponent. The priest would call a "hindrance" to win the point and the participants would laugh about his aggressive play.

"He was a true competitor," Whitmer said.

'America's Guest'

"He also was known as America's guest," Phelps said. Since Fr. Riehle took a vow of poverty when he became a priest, other people typically paid for his meals or golf games, Phelps added.

One example occurred when Phelps coached the Notre Dame basketball team and took a road trip to play the University of Miami. While Phelps and the team held a workout after they arrived to prepare for the game, Fr. Riehle joined an alumnus for a round of golf at Miami Beach's Indian Creek Country Club.

"He loved his cigars," Phelps said. "He loved his golf.

Aside from invitations to dinner and to play either in golf tournaments or at private courses, Fr. Riehle also enjoyed free use of a condominium in Florida in his later years.

Gold-Plated Poverty?

When Fr. Riehle cut back his duties at Notre Dame and semi-retired, he liked to spend the winters away from the frozen conditions in South Bend and in the warmth of Panther Woods in Fort Pierce, Florida. Fr. Riehle's brother Al owned a home at Panther Woods and James Brady and his wife, Fr. Riehle's niece "Nan," bought a condo there in 2000. When Fr. Riehle visited them, a benefactor rented a nearby villa where the priest could stay.

"We used to play a lot of golf," Brady said. "At one time, Jim was an eight handicap."

A keen observer could tell the priest once was a "very good golfer" by the way he hit certain shots, Brady said.

Fr. Riehle also routinely brought out the generosity in others. Brady recalled once going to the cashier at the pro shop at a golf course at Panther Woods where they were about to play a round and started to pay. The fellow behind the counter laughed and said not to even consider paying for Fr. Riehle, since he had the "best deal" of anyone, Brady recalled.

Whether the golf course management, owner or another benefactor made it possible, Fr. Riehle never paid to play golf there. In addition, a friend of Fr. Riehle's arranged for the priest to fly in and out of Florida on private jets. For a priest who took a vow of poverty, Fr. Riehle often traveled in style and played at some of the world's finest golf courses.

"One evening, Jim, Al, Nan and I were to have dinner with Walter and Joan Schilling," Brady recalled. "They were from Maryland and had lived in Panther Woods for some time. Walter has since passed away. We were sitting on the patio having drinks and comparing notes on the great golf courses we had played. I had played a couple, Laurel Valley, some in Hilton Head, etc.; but every time we mentioned a great course in this country or abroad we had not played, Jim had for free. Of course, Jim told the story of playing at one of the old courses in Scotland, mishit his tee shot and asked the caddy—an older fellow—if he could take a mulligan. The caddy replied, 'Of course, Father, but you will be hitting 3.' At that point, we asked Jim how we would go about taking the vow of poverty."

Private Club Connections

Even though he lived in a modest dorm room as a residence hall rector, Fr. Riehle gained exposure to a "pretty opulent lifestyle" due to all of his invitations, said John Gaski, PhD, an associate professor of marketing at Notre Dame's Mendoza College of Business.

Gaski continued, "Some said, 'When Fr. Riehle gets to heaven, it will be a comedown.'"

Fr. Riehle's reputation as a golf aficionado led Gaski to inquire once about where to play.

"I had a Florida conference trip scheduled and asked Fr. Jim if he could recommend any golf courses in the vicinity of my destination," Gaski recalled. "He said, 'Sure. Of course, I only know the private clubs.'"

Fr. Riehle and Smith helped to represent the university by attending a number of Notre Dame alumni golfing events each year. Many of the university's alumni clubs across the country have a golfing fundraiser each summer to help raise scholarship funds for students to attend the school. Events in places such as Chicago, Milwaukee, Indianapolis, Kalamazoo, Michigan, and Toledo, Ohio, were within driving distance of South Bend. The former hockey coach said he enjoyed attending the outings with Fr. Riehle.

Smith, who humorously described himself as "old, fat, bald, mean and crabby," transitioned from coaching the hockey team for 19 seasons to become the manager of Notre Dame's indoor track and football practice facility known as the Loftus Center. The new job did not stop him from remaining part of Fr. Riehle's strong support system, and vice versa.

When the Monogram Club's directors wanted to give Fr. Riehle a salary for his work, he refused the money. As a compromise, the directors offered the avid golfer a membership in the South Bend Country Club. Fr. Riehle accepted and enjoyed many years of friendly golf games and cigar smoking. Access to members of a country club did not hurt the priest's fundraising efforts, either.

"He enjoyed that membership for quite a few years," until the priest's worsening mobility forced him to give up the game, Smith said.

"Once a year, I go to Indiana to bird hunt with my brother, Jack, and our cousin Ed," Brady said. "We time the hunt so that deer season starts the following day. I don't hunt deer, so I would go up to Notre Dame to meet Jim for lunch. Most of the time, lunch was at the University Club. He would have to pay, as I was not a member."

When Fr. Riehle's brother Al heard the story, he seemed jealous, Brady said.

"Al could never remember his brother Jim buying lunch for him," Brady said. "Whenever they went out, Al always paid."

Needless Worry

Fr. Riehle's straightforward manner of communicating did not mesh smoothly with everyone. As occurs in most families, relations with relatives sometimes could be strained by clashing personalities.

Brady, who married Fr. Riehle's niece "Nan" in December 1995, hosted the priest with his wife the following year when he came to visit Greensburg, Pennsylvania, near Pittsburgh. By drinking scotch, smoking cigars and sharing conversation, Fr. Riehle developed a good friendship quickly with Brady, who lived with his wife in a three-story townhouse that had guest bedrooms on the third floor.

It might have been expected, since Fr. Riehle enjoyed a good drink and socializing with the friends who formed his support system. But his niece still worried.

"Nan was concerned that Jim and I would not get along, as she thought Jim could be difficult," Brady said. "From Nan's standpoint, the problem was that Jim did not relate all that well to women. Jim and I had a great time getting to know each other. We spent the evenings sitting on the balcony outside his room, having a scotch and a cigar and just talking. From then on, when he came to Greensburg, he always stayed with us."

Truthful Talk

The coaches' wives had a little gathering at each home football game and Fr. Riehle would drop by to visit. No matter where Fr. Riehle would go, he seemed to be welcomed warmly, said former Notre Dame head football coach Bob Davie, who described the chaplain as a likeable "curmudgeon" and a "regular guy" who just happened to be a priest.

"You looked forward to him saying something," Davie said. "That was his persona."

Fr. Riehle offered "unbiased" opinions, Davie said. He resisted telling people what they wanted to hear and instead told them what they needed to hear. People respected him for telling them the truth, Davie said.

"It was endearing that he could say it and get away with it," Davie said. "That's what was so refreshing."

Hockey Heavyweight

A number of those same friends recalled that the priest played no favorites on the ice when someone got in his way during their pick-up hockey games. Szewczyk, the former engineering professor, recalled receiving jabs from the priest's elbows when they took to the ice at lunchtime to play recreational hockey. They needed to remind themselves almost constantly that Fr. Riehle was a competitive hockey player long before he became a priest. His aggressive style of play surfaced whenever Fr. Riehle stepped onto the ice for the pick-up games.

Even with multiple and frequent warnings to stop the rough play, Fr. Riehle found himself unable to moderate his instinctive competitiveness. The bumps and bruises that he inflicted on the other participants ultimately healed, while the friendships between the players grew. The personal relationships also might have benefitted when Fr. Riehle ultimately agreed to stop lacing up his skates for the lunchtime games.

Despite absorbing the priest's on-ice body checks, Szewczyk became a close friend of Fr. Riehle and later served as one of the pallbearers at the priest's well-attended funeral.

'Fr. Cheapshot'

Fr. Riehle picked up the nickname "Fr. Cheapshot" from those who wanted to tease him about his rugged play in recreational ice hockey games for Notre Dame's staff members. Those games ignited his competitive instincts. The priest was not at all reluctant to play in a way that people knowledgeable about the sport might admire. However, rival players who ended up knocked off of their skates and sprawled out on the ice after receiving one of the clergyman's body checks acknowledged occasionally thinking of names to call him other than "reverend." They ultimately settled on poking fun at his hard-hitting play with the nickname "Fr. Cheapshot." If the intent was to encourage Fr. Riehle to tone down his on-ice aggressiveness, it failed.

One of the participants in the men's hockey games was Smith, who arrived at Notre Dame to launch its varsity hockey program during 1968. Fr. Riehle was one of the first people that Smith met on campus and they became good friends by traveling with the school's hockey team on numerous road trips across the Midwest. Smith, who coached the hockey team between 1968 and 1987, was among those who learned firsthand that Fr. Riehle could pack a wallop. No one was off limits. Even Parseghian, who was Notre Dame's esteemed football coach at the time, was dropped to the ice by one of Fr. Riehle's clean but bruising checks.

Indeed, an article in the *South Bend* (Indiana) *Tribune* actually called him "Fr. Cheapshot." The nickname amused his sister Joan.

"In fact, I still have the newspaper article about him that called him Fr. Cheapshot," Joan said. "I think it's funny."

When asked if Fr. Riehle truly deserved a nickname given to a competitor who exerts force in situations when it may not be required, his good friend Szewczyk replied "yes," without any hesitation.

"We were playing a lunchtime hockey game," Szewczyk said. The intent was to create a pleasant atmosphere for "camaraderie" and exercise, not to knock the other faculty and staff members into the boards, the retired engineering professor added.

"Jim would use his elbow and things like that," Szewczyk said. "You never wanted to get hit by Jim."

Szewczyk talked as if he still had vivid memories of absorbing the impact of checks given by the priest several decades ago.

"He would cross that line to just where he could get away with it," Szewczyk said in describing Fr. Riehle and his on-ice aggressiveness.

On-ice Intensity

The rough play would spark the competitive fires of Paul Shoults, a former Notre Dame defensive backfield coach during the Ara Parseghian era.

"Paul would go after Father," if the chaplain knocked the coach off of the puck, Szewczyk said.

If Fr. Riehle checked Shoults into the boards, the football coach would respond in kind. Both were good and physical players who were pretty evenly matched.

"They each had fuses that were about a quarter of an inch long," Smith recalled. "Of course, if they'd get bumped or something, they immediately wanted to retaliate. This was not supposed to be that type of a program."

Greatest Hits

"Eventually, we suggested to him that he… maybe think about hanging it up because it wouldn't look good to have a priest in the middle of a Pier Six brawl," Smith said.

Fortunately, the Pier Six brawls that occurred on New York's Staten Island generations ago between bare-knuckled boxers never were reenacted by members of the Notre Dame men's faculty hockey team.

But with a slippery and unforgiving playing surface, tumbles to the ice during the action were not unusual. The contact typically was relatively minor and caused by skating missteps. Other than Fr. Riehle and two hockey coaches, none of the men skated especially well or had played much hockey.

"The rest of them were rather wobbly," Smith said. "Of course, a lot of times they would run into one another, not in a mean-spirited fashion but just by accident."

Sharp Elbows, Quick Stick

When Notre Dame started a varsity hockey program in 1968, faculty league hockey would take place on Tuesdays and Thursdays on the campus ice rink. Fr. Riehle enjoyed playing in those games and participants literally felt his presence on the ice.

"When he laced them up, he came out to play and out to win," Whitmer said. "There was no compromise."

Fr. Riehle had "sharp elbows and he had a quick stick," Whitmer added.

"You wouldn't expect that from a man of the cloth," Whitmer said.

Carberry's Comic Relief

One of Fr. Riehle's fellow recreational hockey players was esteemed chemical engineering professor James Carberry. Amid the hotly contested play of some of the participants, Carberry brought an admirable desire to take part but he lacked the skill level of the others. He also faced other challenges that he tried to overcome, without much success.

Carberry had "very bad eye sight" and wore thick eyeglasses that he tried to protect by removing them when he played hockey, Szewczyk said.

Without his glasses, Carberry could not see where the puck went and his plan to listen for it in the midst of stick noises and the sound of skate blades against the ice failed. He became an unintentional source of amusement for his friends as he fruitlessly attempted to hear the sound of the puck and skate to where he thought it was going. It was not unusual for Carberry to take off in one direction, while others on the ice who actually could see the puck skated the other way.

Lunch Pals

Carberry became a good friend of Fr. Riehle by organizing group lunches after returning to his alma mater to start a second career as a professor after leaving Dupont, where he served as a top chemical engineer and inventor.

Also a graduate of Yale University, Carberry wanted to bring that school's networking traditions to Notre Dame. He enjoyed going to the Yale Club in New York and meeting his pals for meals, so he spearheaded the formation of a similar group at Notre Dame. He named it the Algonquin Table to reflect the diversity of those who attended the gatherings, much the way an eclectic group of journalists, editors, actors, authors and press agents convened on a regular basis at the Algonquin Hotel in New York for about 10 years starting in June 1919.

When Smith came to Notre Dame to coach the school's fledgling hockey team in 1968, Fr. Riehle served as the dean of students and they became part of Carberry's group by eating lunch together almost every day at the University Club with roughly a dozen other Notre Dame employees. The meals let Fr. Riehle bond with the university's head accountant, athletic department staffers, academic faculty members and others from a public television station, WNDU, owned by the university at the time.

The Algonquin Table was a "big part" of Fr. Riehle's life, Phelps said. The all-male group gathered with the priest each day for lunch and became an integral part of his support system.

"He lived for that [camaraderie] every day at lunch," Phelps said.

Table Manners

Former Notre Dame President Fr. Edward "Monk" Malloy knew about the group but said he never received an invitation to join the Algonquin Table for lunch.

"I think they were happier not to have any top administrators around," Fr. Malloy said. "Plus, they were, you might say, a fairly conservative crowd.

It was better for them to have a chance to ventilate, or share their opinions, about whatever they might think."

Despite Fr. Riehle's conservative views, Fr. Malloy said he never considered the sports chaplain to be "disloyal" or a "threat" in any way.

"He just had his own opinions," Fr. Malloy said. "Most of the time, we would just agree to disagree."

Fr. Malloy said he and Fr. Riehle never got into any sustained arguments.

Unexpected Guest

Before the Notre Dame University Club closed and forced the Algonquin Table to move its lunches elsewhere, a female reporter from the *South Bend* (Indiana) *Tribune* called Smith for permission to join the attendees for lunch. She expressed interest in writing an article about the group in hopes of saving the club. No one told Fr. Riehle, who was accustomed to only men gathering for the lunches. After all, Fr. Riehle and his lunchtime buddies had been eating together without women since the days when Notre Dame served an all-male student population.

When Fr. Riehle first spotted the female reporter sitting at the table with all of the men who usually joined him for lunch, it probably seemed to the priest as if a woman had just entered the men's locker room. Fr. Riehle reacted accordingly. It occurred at a time later in Fr. Riehle's life when the infirmities of age required him to hobble into the room before he reacted with his characteristic bluntness.

"What in the hell is she doing here," Fr. Riehle inquired of his lunch companions. His colleagues explained that she had been invited to observe an Algonquin Table lunch to gain an appreciation of the group's collegiality that could be shared with the newspaper's readers in hopes of preventing the University Club from shutting down.

That lunch became an awkward one for Fr. Riehle, who came from the ranks of men who had served in the military and spoke frankly among themselves, but tried to mind their language and manners in the company of women. Gentility at the all-male lunches usually gave way to directness among the friends who attended regularly. The chaplain never appeared to his friends that he was able to relax that day in the presence of the female reporter who was attempting to chronicle the lunch for the newspaper's readers.

Motor City U-Turn

Not only was Fr. Riehle someone you wanted on your side during a competition or a battle of any kind, he also could provide seasoned counsel in matters of the heart. His understanding about the human frailties and emotions of young people looking for love was derived in part through personal experience.

His pre-seminary life reached a turning point when he took a job with his father's former employer, Shelby SalesBook, and moved to Detroit. While living in the Motor City, Jim nearly deviated from his eventual path to the priesthood.

"That's when he met the girl he fell for," his sister Joan said. "I never met her and I don't know her name. I may have known it back then but we are talking the early '50s or late '40s. The story is very interesting."

Smitten Salesman

The woman who attracted his attention was a widow who had a very young son, Joan said. The smitten brother told his sister that he decided to ask for his girlfriend's hand in marriage. On his way to visit her, he stopped in church to say a prayer and seek the Lord's guidance with his pivotal decision. Upon exiting the church, he set his mind solely on marrying and having a family, she said.

"That was just so important to him, but he knew that God wanted him to be a priest," Joan said. He came to that realization while praying in church prior to proposing to his girlfriend. But he tried to ignore what he had discerned and instead focused on following through with his plan to present his sweetheart with an engagement ring.

"He went and asked her and she turned him down," Joan said her brother told her. "So, that was the end of that."

Unrequited Love

While numerous people described how Fr. Riehle performed his priestly duties capably for anyone who needed him, his friends noticed that he seemed to prefer socializing with men rather than women. His best friends speculated that it stemmed from the deep disappointment that he endured before deciding to enter the seminary when his romance fizzled out.

Largely unknown to all but his closest friends and family members was the part of his past in which he courted and fell in love when he worked as a salesman. The rejection of his marriage proposal was the kind of stinging rebuff that a person likely never forgets but ultimately learns to accept, along with any emotional scars that are hidden beneath the surface.

"He was jilted," Szewczyk said the future priest acknowledged to him. The personal blow was a double-whammy. A soft-hearted man lost the woman who he loved and the end of their relationship meant that he also would not become the father of her young son. If she had accepted the proposal, the single mother would have received a husband and her son would have gained a dad. It seemed like a perfect match to the gentleman who had proposed. But God apparently had other plans.

Since the priest confided to his family and close friends that he stopped in a church to pray before he visited his then-girlfriend to propose, it did not surprise anyone that he was rebuffed after sensing the answer that God tried to convey to him through his prayers was not to follow through with his plan; it was doomed to fail. But the heart and spirit of a determined man are difficult to assuage. The same man who instinctively knocked down his closest friends in recreational hockey games was not going to give up the love of his life without letting her have the choice.

That moment became a crossroads in his life. Rather than put himself in situations that would remind him of a love who was lost, Fr. Riehle seemed to prefer socializing with his buddies, who accepted his disagreeable moments, occasional brusqueness and other foibles, while valuing his positive qualities far more than his shortcomings.

The rejection of his proposal, as disappointing as it was for him to hear, ultimately cleared the way for him to pursue his priestly vocation that led to his more than four decades of service at Notre Dame until his death on October 29, 2008.

His experience of losing the love of his life also gave him an unusually perceptive view of relationships to aid those who sought his assistance in matters of romance. As the head of discipline, he also needed to mete out punishment and determine its severity for those who violated university policies about fraternizing with members of the opposite sex on campus during the sexually charged 1960s and 1970s.

When such instances arose, he possessed a special insight from his personal experiences that aided him.

Father to a Flock

The chaplain became an undisputed father figure for Notre Dame students and athletes. He helped to guide them through what may have been the university's most revolutionary period. However, Fr. Riehle possessed first-hand knowledge about the challenges of dating and building relationships that he could use to guide the students who came to him for advice.

Certain people seem so well suited for a given role in this world that no substitute could ever truly do the job as well. The latter description might best reflect Fr. Riehle's value to Notre Dame and all of the people there who depended on him during his decades of service.

Casual observers initially might be put off by the priest's "gruff, rough" demeanor, but those who knew him well can attest that he genuinely had a "heart of gold," Szewczyk said.

Chapter 3

SHARE A SENSE
OF HUMOR

Laughter is a great elixir to reduce stress, to add to enjoyment in life and to build relationships. Psychology studies have found that a sense of humor enhances mental health. Fr. Riehle appreciated humor and did not mind people slinging funny verbal jabs in his direction, since he was adept at responding in kind in his own deadpan style. Despite hardships in his life, Fr. Riehle was a consummate practitioner of the art of helping others to laugh and to have fun.

Humor also is effective in reaching out to people who otherwise may be distracted by anxiety. The use of humor is a valuable way to gain trust and friendships, as well as ease tensions. In addition, laughter transcends race, ethnic background and social status. Fr. Riehle understood the value of humor and shared it openly.

Langston Hughes, an African-American poet, playwright, columnist and novelist who gained acclaim during the "Harlem Renaissance" period of the 1920s, wrote, "Like a welcome summer rain, humor may suddenly cleanse and cool the earth, the air and you."

Fr. Riehle's sharp wit might even have been more welcome than a summer rain, since it helped people under extreme pressure gain precious enjoyment in life at times when stratospheric expectations might seem impossible to achieve. In many cases, a joke from Fr. Riehle at a critical moment turned a tense time into a happy one. The result could be the lifting of worry and a renewed focus on seizing the opportunity that lies ahead.

In the words of former U.S. President and five-star World War II General Dwight D. Eisenhower, "A sense of humor is part of the art of leadership, of getting along with people, of getting things done."

Quick Quips

Fr. Riehle's seriousness in performing his duties contrasted with his legendary sense of humor. His quick quips could catch listeners by surprise.

"He had a great sense of humor," said Marty Allen, a Notre Dame graduate, a former football team manager and a past leader of the university's Monogram Club. "It was a very different sense of humor. He liked to laugh and he liked to kid people an awful lot."

"He had a dry sense of humor, too," Phelps said. "He'd just lay it out there and you'd get it and laugh."

Fr. Riehle's deadpan sense of humor gained national attention when Adidas teamed him up with Joe Montana for a television commercial. The priest delivered the punch line when he asked the four-time Super Bowl champion with the San Francisco 49ers what he had done since leaving Notre Dame. The chaplain's humor shined through during that moment on camera but he only was acting when he delivered his funniest line. The script called for him to convey that he had lost touch with Montana's post-Notre Dame success as a professional football player. But the priest actually prided himself on staying in touch and available to former players and students when they left the university and later returned to visit.

Padre's Punch Line

In the television commercial, Fr. Riehle began to reminisce with Montana, who was shown visiting the campus years after his graduation.

"Joe, do you remember that great pass that you threw?" Fr. Riehle asked.

"The one against the Cowboys in the playoffs," replied Montana, who was enshrined in the Pro Football Hall of Fame in 2000 and was hinting at a touchdown pass he drew to receiver Dwight Clark as the quarterback of the San Francisco 49ers against Dallas in the 1981 NFC Championship Game.

"No, Joe, the one against Houston in the Cotton Bowl," Fr. Riehle responded incredulously, as if nothing other than a Notre Dame game mattered. The game against Houston was Montana's last as a collegian and it certainly was unforgettable. He rallied his team from a 22-point fourth-quarter deficit by overcoming the flu, strong winds and ice to win 35-34. Montana threw the game-winning, eight-yard touchdown pass to receiver David "Kris" Haines on the final play with no time left on the game clock.

After a reflective pause, Fr. Riehle asked Montana another question.

"What did you ever end up doing after you left college?" the priest asked facetiously. Of course, Fr. Riehle, an avid football fan, knew Montana had become a professional football star who ultimately won four Super Bowls, three Super Bowl MVP awards and two consecutive Associated Press MVP awards for the 1989 and 1990 seasons.

Cape Crusaders?

Fr. Riehle became the target of good-natured kidding whenever members of his family thought his status seemed a little too exalted. If a discussion was taking place and he was speaking with the authority of a learned religious man, they quickly responded by performing an exaggerated mannerism intended to poke fun at him and draw laughter.

"That was the big joke in the family," his sister Joan Riehle Ruse said. "It was just hysterical."

When first ordained as a priest, Fr. Riehle wore a long, close-fitting garment known as a cassock that had a black, shoulder cape that reached to his elbows. If he started talking in a manner that ever seemed to them that he might be pontificating, at least one or possibly more of the family members would shimmy his or her shoulders as if to make an imaginary cape flap ostentatiously.

"They'd all pretend that they were flipping their cape back over their shoulder and he'd see them doing that," his sister said. "Then he'd start to laugh and he'd quit."

It became a family ritual and Fr. Riehle appeared to laugh as hard as anyone else when it happened. Even as the years passed, the occasional use of the comedic gesture remained funny for all of the members of the family. Everyone always laughed.

"I have no idea why it was so funny to Jim," Joan said. "Anyway, whenever he'd start talking about anything important or anything serious, they would all start doing this. He would start to laugh and that would be the end of it."

He then knew it was time to tone down whatever he was saying.

"Actually, I don't think Jim was ever like that but they just wanted to tease him," his sister said.

Joan has a photo of her brother Jim wearing the cape when he was first ordained but he seldom wore the cape in the following years.

His family members may have helped him to develop an attitude of detachment from trying to preach to anyone and it could have been one of the key reasons people considered him so approachable. It also was instant fun for the family when adults in the same room with Fr. Riehle started to flip their imaginary capes.

John Wayne Impersonator

Former Notre Dame linebacker Ed "Duke" Scales received his nickname during his freshman year, 1970-1971, when he dressed like a cowboy to impersonate famed actor John Wayne, who was best known for portraying "good guy" characters in movies about the Old West. Wayne also possibly was the most celebrated person ever to have the nickname "Duke."

Scales began to be called "Duke" by his classmates after he portrayed Wayne in the university's traditional AnTostal event. The word AnTostal is Gaelic for "the festival" and is used to describe a series of activities that have been held at Notre Dame during the last week of the academic year each spring since 1967. The aim is to let students have fun before preparing for final exams and leaving school for the summer. As part of a skit, Scales and a sidekick wanted to ride horses to an outdoor stage where the performances would take place.

"I had to go see Fr. Riehle to get it cleared to bring a couple horses on campus, since he was the dean of students at the time," Duke said. "I remember him looking across his desk, smoking that cigar and asking, 'You want to what??!!' After giving me his obligatory hard time, and reminding me we would be required to clean up all the horse dung, he gave me the okay. That was 40 years ago now, and I still remember it well!"

Levity for Losers

A favorite one-liner that Fr. Riehle used at just about every annual Monogram Club banquet for many years typically could be heard on Thursday during reunion weekend, shortly after an annual golf tournament that awarded prizes to the top three teams.

"After announcing the first, second and third place winners of the outing, he [Fr. Riehle] would yell out the names of the fourth place team and shout, 'no prize,'" recalled Tom "Big T" Ross, a former defensive tackle on the football team who graduated from Notre Dame in 1974. "It was classic and cracked up everybody at the banquet."

Ross, now a realtor in Phoenix, Arizona, arrived at Notre Dame as a scholarship football player and played on the university's freshman football team before his athletic career ended prematurely due to a series of back surgeries. Not able to win a varsity letter on the playing field, Ross received an honorary one as a surprise at the June 1999 banquet of the Monogram Club. Fr. Riehle and Scales, a former football teammate, presented the monogram. Ross described Scales, a Monogram Club winner, as his best friend since their college years at Notre Dame.

"After they took the picture, he [Fr. Riehle] said, '*...make sure you pay your dues, Ross...*' He loved dues-paying members," Ross said.

Despite his good deed as an adult, Scales laid no claim to perfection as a collegian.

"I didn't burn any couches, though," Scales interjected.

Bedazzled Dancer

Professor John Gaski recalled entering the Torch Lounge in South Bend near the Notre Dame campus with two classmates one night when he was a graduate student in 1973. Known for staying open late when other places would be closed, the night club featured female dancers who also fraternized with the patrons.

When the three graduate students walked into the club and sat down, they looked across the room and noticed that a dancer was on the lap of a gentleman who resembled Fr. Riehle. Upon a closer look, Gaski said he suddenly realized it *is* Fr. Riehle. The priest had stopped by for a drink with then-athletic trainer "Big John" Whitmer and a coach as part of an evening of holiday celebration. Among all of the gentlemen in the club, Fr. Riehle was the one who the dancer chose to give some attention.

"When he noticed us Notre Dame grad students looking over at him, he came by and said the immortal and poignant words, 'I'm just scouting the local talent for you guys.'"

To Gaski, the priest's reaction was priceless.

"It was a great Notre Dame moment," Gaski said, "and totally innocent on Fr. Riehle's part. And there is no way he would mind public reporting of the episode, I'll bet."

Ever one to keep his sense of humor, Fr. Riehle did not disappoint that night with his quick retort.

"It was a humorous, ironic, picturesque moment for all of us," Gaski recalled.

Empty Lap Surprise

Decades later, Whitmer said he had no trouble remembering that unforgettable evening when the dancer took the words about finding an "empty lap" literally from the award-winning Broadway musical *Hello Dolly!* The occasion was Dyngus Day in South Bend, which is held the day after Easter as a Polish heritage celebration. Many eating and drinking establishments gave out free food as part of the tradition of revelry.

On that Dyngus Day, the dancer chose Fr. Riehle to share a moment of fun when the priest and several of his friends dropped by for a late-night drink. Lap dances had not been invented but the dancer still amused her patrons by sitting briefly on Fr. Riehle's lap.

Fr. Riehle's group started out that night by going to a bar on the city's west side called Marion's Hideaway, which Whitmer said had the best cabbage rolls of "anyplace in town." They next headed to Joe's Bar to enjoy Polish ham, hard boiled eggs and steamed Polish sausage, also known as kielbasa.

"Then we went to another bar called Albert's," Whitmer said. "From there, at about midnight, we decided to go to the Torch and we walked in. We got about 10 feet from the door and this one entertainer yelled out, "Fr. Riehle, how are you?"

A somewhat "sheepish look" came over Fr. Riehle's face, as if the chaplain knew he would never live that moment down, said Whitmer, who roared with laughter when recalling the story.

"He knew what was out there because he had been in the real world for a while," Whitmer said. "He was a pretty astute guy."

The dancer came over to speak with Fr. Riehle.

Glory Days

"I'm sure he didn't frequent the place," Whitmer said. The group's visit to the lounge was sort of "a lark" to finish an evening of celebration that he recalled began at 7 p.m.

Dyngus Day, which celebrates the end of the season of Lent, was a "big deal" in South Bend decades ago as a holiday to honor Polish-American culture, heritage and traditions.

South Bend has commemorated Dyngus Day for more than 80 years. Presidential candidate Bobby Kennedy visited on Dyngus Day in 1968, while former President Bill Clinton dropped by to meet revelers in 2008. Since the first party held at South Bend's West Side Democratic Club in 1930, the popularity of Dyngus Day grew and led to celebrations at social and union halls, private clubs, bars and restaurants.

Dyngus Day lost luster in later years when the giving away of free food stopped, the price of drinks went up and law enforcement intervened due to drinking-related accidents, Whitmer said.

"Plus, the old Polish neighborhoods of the first and second generations" faded and a core group of interest in the festivities waned, Whitmer said.

Dyngus Day in South Bend still is "fun," even though it has downsized since its peak, said Whitmer, who joined with Fr. Riehle in celebrating despite the German ethnicity that they shared. Even South Bend's African-American community began to endorse the celebration in 1971 and called it "Solidarity Day."

As that memorable evening in 1973 showed, Fr. Riehle could take a joke well but he also had a knack of delivering a quick retort, Whitmer said.

"He was just a genuinely good, fun guy to be around," Whitmer said. "And the difference between him and the rest of us is that he wore a collar and his mission in life was the priesthood."

Another Nickname

Fr. Riehle, also known as "Reels" to his friends, understood that people liked to laugh. He tried to put his sense of humor to good use.

For example, he might interject humor when disciplining a student for a minor transgression. That technique still allowed the priest to make his point and eased the stress level for someone who broke one of the rules.

Fr. Riehle's pre-seminary experiences enhanced his role as a clergyman. One instance involved a university staffer who worked in the athletic department.

Dean of Discipline

Sports team trainer, John Markovich, served as a Navy corpsman in Vietnam before he became a 23-year-old freshman. Markovich lived in the football stadium during the fall of 1971 and enjoyed hosting parties at his place on the weekends when the football team did not play a home game.

The chance to party at Notre Dame Stadium apparently proved to be difficult for Markovich's guests and their friends to pass up.

One night after a home football game, a football-playing friend of Markovich's had more than 20 relatives and friends in town. They gathered at the player's dorm room to celebrate a Notre Dame win. Students could drink alcohol in their rooms but not in the hallway. In this instance, far too many people came to fit everyone into a dorm room built for four students.

A priest who was the rector at that dorm became aware of the party and approached the host to warn him that he would call Fr. Riehle, then the dean of students, if any of the partygoers remained in the hallway with alcohol.

Markovich intervened and invited all 30 people to his room at Notre Dame Stadium. His room once served as the visiting coaches' locker room but no longer was used for that purpose. Instead, referees used it at halftime during home football games to receive refreshments from Notre Dame's team managers. The rest of each week, Markovich had a private room and access to the entire stadium. He was attending Notre Dame courtesy of the GI bill and receiving free room and board as an athletic trainer. Markovich also personalized his living space.

"I put a bar in front of the shower," Markovich said. "I had a refrigerator in the shower and a big, six-foot Hamm's beer sign above the shower, with an Irish flag above the sign."

'Stadium Club' Celebration

Markovich's friends called his room the "Stadium Club."

Fr. Riehle previously had cautioned Markovich not to have any big parties because noise would echo from the stadium and cause a disturbance.

With 30-some people heading to the stadium to party and others joining in, the group that night turned into a boisterous crowd.

After about an hour of revelry in Notre Dame Stadium, a campus security officer showed up at the room. Markovich recalled the following dialog.

Markovich asked, "Is there a problem, officer?"

The officer said, "I was just told to say Fr. Riehle sent me."

Markovich responded, "The party's over."

The officer replied, "That's what Fr. Riehle said you'd say. There's no problem."

At next Monday's football practice two days later, Fr. Riehle took time to smoke some cigars and ultimately ended up next to Markovich.

Fr. Riehle said, "It must have been a hell of a party."

"Yep," Markovich replied.

Markovich served as the basketball team's athletic trainer during Phelps' first two years at the helm of the school's program. After that, Markovich left to attend pharmacy school at Creighton University in Omaha, Nebraska. Markovich now owns and operates City Pharmacy, of Slater, Missouri, where the late actor Steve McQueen lived as a boy.

'Magic' Mass

Phelps only became angry with Fr. Riehle one time, the former coach wrote in his book, "Digger Phelps's Tales from the Notre Dame Hardwood." Notre Dame was going to play Michigan State and "Magic" Johnson for a berth in the 1979 NCAA Basketball tournament's Final Four. The NCAA put Notre Dame's basketball team in a hotel that was inundated with Michigan State fans. During the stay, Fr. Riehle became friendly with a number of Michigan State supporters by talking with them in the hotel's lobby. The regional final between the two teams was scheduled on a Sunday and Fr. Riehle organized a Mass to take place in a hotel meeting room.

The Notre Dame basketball team usually had a fairly intimate pre-game Mass for the players, coaches and support staffers. However, word spread about the planned religious service among the fans at the hotel and the chance to celebrate a Mass with the Notre Dame sports chaplain proved enticing.

Michigan State fans were "everywhere," Phelps wrote. Some of them even brought pom-poms, he added.

Phelps recalled approaching Fr. Riehle about the Mass attracting so many fans for his team's opponent that day. He suggested scheduling a second Mass just for the "Michigan State sinners" and including an offertory to raise some money.

But as a priest, Fr. Riehle ultimately needed to answer not only to a coach, but to the Lord. In that spirit, Fr. Riehle welcomed everyone to the Mass who wanted to worship, regardless of allegiances to a particular team.

Michigan State, led by Johnson and fellow future NBA player Greg Kelser, won the game that day 80-68. The Spartans culminated their tournament run by beating Indiana State and its star Larry Bird to win the 1979 national championship.

Phelps's Conversion

Ironically, Phelps later became an ESPN basketball analyst and apparently warmed up to the Spartans in the intervening years. To promote a televised prime-time match-up on ESPNs College GameDay in East Lansing between host Michigan State and its intrastate rival Michigan on January 25, 2014, Phelps dressed from the waist up as "Sparty," a bronze statue that stands as an iconic campus landmark.

"This is Sparta," Phelps shouted with his face painted bronze while wearing a costume that exhibited the rippling abdominal muscles on "Sparty's" muscular physique.

A further connection with the 1979 Spartans team for that 2014 game is that Michigan State wore "retro" jerseys from Nike to commemorate those used by Magic Johnson's national championship squad coached by fiery "Jud" Heathcote, who mentored his successor, Tom Izzo. If Fr. Riehle would have been alive to see Phelps dress and talk as "Sparty," the chaplain likely would have been amused at the ironic image of the former Notre Dame coach who had objected to Michigan State's fans attending a game-day Mass 35 years earlier. Fr. Riehle would have appreciated the humor in the situation as much as anyone.

Celebrating with Celebrities

When Notre Dame's celebrity fans would visit the school, every one of them seemingly would want to stop by and talk to Fr. Riehle, athletic department administrator Jim Fraleigh said. The visitors wanted to hear stories about Notre Dame and its rich history.

Fraleigh witnessed a stream of people visiting Fr. Riehle, since anyone coming to meet with the priest needed to pass by Fraleigh's office and the desk of the secretary that worked for both of them.

On the Fridays before home football games, the number of people who would drop by to spend time, to laugh and to reminisce with Fr. Riehle was "amazing," Fraleigh said. As a result, Fraleigh joked that he never managed to get much work done on those Fridays.

"He'd always call me in," Fraleigh said. Fr. Riehle reveled in introducing Fraleigh to everybody who visited and in sharing memories with all of them.

"It used to just be a day of storytelling," Fraleigh said. Everybody seemed to have a special Fr. Riehle story to share.

The anecdotes touched on every aspect of life and it was "really spectacular" to have the privilege to hear them, Fraleigh said. Years after Fr. Riehle's death, happy memories of those stories and the sound of laughter that they produced remain.

Dan the Man!

It seemed fitting that Dan Gibbs Jr., a member of Notre Dame's class of 1967, became the namesake of the annual golf tournament in Chicago held by its local alumni club because he organized the event to raise scholarship money for students before he succumbed to cancer. The tournament, renamed the Daniel S. Gibbs Memorial golf outing for many years, takes place annually at the Butterfield Country Club in Oakbrook Terrace, Illinois.

Before Gibbs took the reins of the event and boosted the entry fee from $50 to $300, the revenues collected did not leave much for scholarships after paying for the tournament's expenses, his brother Greg Gibbs said. Fr. Riehle accepted invitations each year to play as a guest of the organizers.

One year, par 3 holes were featured in a special contest. Any participant who struck a hole-in-one at one of those holes would win a new car. The prize at one hole was a Cadillac. Another hole offered a chance to win a Chevrolet Camaro. Only one par 3 hole was not part of the contest. That particular fairway is where Fr. Riehle fulfilled a golfer's dream by hitting a hole-in-one. Many golfers would consider that achievement to be a sportsman's Holy Grail.

But Fr. Riehle's competitive spirit caused him to have a somewhat different reaction. Since hole-in-one accomplishments are rare and winning a new car as a prize for hitting one are even more odds-defying, human nature got the best of Fr. Riehle. He began "grousing" about not winning a car, Greg Gibbs said. Whether Fr. Riehle actually needed a car or may have given it away was not the point. Rather than celebrating his hole-in-one, which many good golfers never achieve in a lifetime, Fr. Riehle's frustration surfaced as he expressed his disappointment about not winning a vehicle.

"He was going on and on about it, and he just couldn't let it go," said Greg Gibbs, who added that he sat at a table with Fr. Riehle after the golf tournament and personally witnessed the priest voice his displeasure.

Krause Stops Grouse

Finally, Edward "Moose" Krause, who by then had retired as Notre Dame's athletic director, heard enough. He reminded Fr. Riehle that other people had paid for the open bar and the food that they were enjoying. But Krause was far from finished.

"You mooched a ride off of me to get here," Greg Gibbs recalled Krause adding in his rebuttal to the priest. "And, you'll be coming back with me, unless you keep complaining and then you can walk."

With South Bend about 50 miles away from the country club, Krause's response to the complaints served a dual-purpose effect of quieting down Fr. Riehle and entertaining the people at their table with his retort.

Father vs. Father

Dan Gibbs Sr., the father of Greg Gibbs and Dan Gibbs Jr., graduated from Notre Dame in 1938 along with Moose Krause. The elder Gibbs was a standout athlete but Fr. Riehle had no way of knowing that the senior citizen who attended Monogram Club events in his golden years had been a Notre Dame letter winner. That achievement gave the Gibbs family patriarch the right to become a Monogram Club member. Fr. Riehle mistakenly assumed that Dan Gibbs Sr. felt entitled to attend the club's events because of his late son Dan's membership. Never one to overlook a rule, Fr. Riehle was serving as the executive director of the organization when he approached the elderly gentleman about the situation.

Greg Gibbs recalled Fr. Riehle telling his dad, "Dan, just because your son was a member of the club doesn't mean that you are eligible to attend."

Anyone Fr. Riehle ever challenged about anything likely wished to have had justification as compelling as the one that Dan Gibbs Sr. offered. While his son, Dan Jr., was injured during his sophomore year, seldom played afterward and became a student athletic director during his senior year with the responsibility of coordinating free tickets, Dan Sr. had been a Notre Dame athletic star. The elder Dan Gibbs was a top performer in both football and track and field.

Olympic-Sized Error

"Dad had been selected for 1940 U.S. Olympic Team in the pole vault," Greg Gibbs said. "Fr. Riehle was hooking horns with the wrong guy."

Unfortunately, the outbreak of World War II led to the cancellation of the Olympic Games that year and again in 1944. Only in 1948, after the hostilities had ended, did the Olympics resume. Dan Gibbs Sr. never had the chance to compete in the Olympics but winning a varsity letter gave him the right to enjoy Notre Dame's Monogram Club activities.

If there had been no war and the Olympics had been held, Dan Gibbs Sr. would have had an even better story to share with Fr. Riehle.

Scrambled Egg Experiment

Fr. Riehle liked to tell funny stories as much as hear them. One of the humorous stories involved his own mother. She ultimately became a terrific cook but did not begin her married life that way.

As a newlywed, Fr Riehle's mother tried to please her husband by honoring his request to make scrambled eggs for breakfast. Unfortunately, she had no experience cooking eggs that way, so she attempted to improvise.

She knew how to make soft-boiled eggs, so she tried to use that technique in an ill-fated experiment to scramble the eggs unconventionally. She put the unbroken eggs in a pot, heated the water to a boil and tried shaking them with a spoon to scramble them.

"She was trying to scramble them in their shells," family friend Marty Allen said. Not surprisingly, the desired effect was not achieved but it gave the family an amusing story to share that has outlived both the mother and her son.

Tomato Taste

During a visit to see Allen in Grand Rapids, Fr. Riehle stopped by just before lunchtime. Allen's wife had been to the market earlier that day and purchased fresh tomatoes.

"My wife was about to fix a little lunch," Allen recalled. She offered to make a bacon and tomato sandwich for Fr. Riehle and mentioned she also would do so for her husband.

"Don't go out of your way," Fr. Riehle told her. His initial reluctance to accept the offer eased a few moments later when Fr. Riehle spoke again. Mrs. Allen listened attentively to his revised instructions.

James Riehle, 15, on the left, poses with his mother, "Tillie," 36, sister Joan, 8, and brother Al, 13, in Saginaw, Michigan.

This photo from approximately 1942 shows Jim Riehle as a student at St. Andrew's High School in Saginaw.

James serves in the U.S. Army during the Korean Conflict in the 1950s.

He wears a cassock in the early 1960s as he transitioned from a deacon to a priest.

Fr. Riehle receives his master's of business administration diploma from
Notre Dame in 1978.

A youthful-looking Fr. Riehle did not
become a priest until age 39.

Fr. Riehle displayed a look of confidence
that he could instill in the players,
Joe Theismann said.

Fr. Riehle loved buffets.

Fr. Riehle beams along with President Gerald R. Ford, a former University of Michigan football star, who received an honorary Notre Dame monogram.

Fr. Riehle, his sister Joan, mother Tillie, and brother Al enjoy visiting together in Florida.

This photo from approximately 1970 shows the chaplain in football coach Ara Parseghian's office.

The 1988 national championship team gathers around Head Coach Lou Holtz, with Fr. Edward "Monk" Malloy and Fr. Riehle to the right.

A referee, Lou Holtz and Fr. Riehle watch the action on the field during a football game.

Fr. Riehle provided a reassuring spiritual presence for Notre Dame players and coaches.

Frs. Mark Poorman, Bill Beauchamp, Riehle and Malloy pose happily with an "angel."

This collage shows Fr. Riehle and special moments from his Notre Dame career to celebrate his 80th birthday.

Fr. Riehle props himself up on his cane as he stands on Notre Dame's sideline.

Golf and cigar smoking were two of Fr. Riehle's favorite activities.

Fr. Riehle enjoys a cigar as he sits on Notre Dame's bench–possibly to savor a win.

The chaplain watches Notre Dame's football team.

Former football coach Charlie Weis, former Athletic Director Dick Rosenthal, women's Basketball Coach, Muffet McGraw, men's Basketball Coach, Mike Brey, as well as former football coaches Lou Holtz, Gerry Faust and Ara Parseghian, attend Fr. Riehle's October 2008 funeral Mass at Notre Dame.

Former basketball coach Richard "Digger" Phelps lauds Fr. Riehle's service as a chaplain.

"By the way, when my mother used to make me a bacon and tomato sandwich, she used to put a fried egg on top of it," Fr. Riehle said.

The suggestion amused Allen and his wife.

"He thought maybe all of the sudden that she was a short order cook," Allen said.

Allen and his wife welcomed the priest as their guest during events at Notre Dame and for home visits.

"We were delighted to have him," Allen said.

Kicker's Jumbo Jersey

Fr. Riehle enjoyed humor as much as anyone and one such moment of levity came during Ara Parseghian's tenure as Notre Dame's coach when a walk-on kicker named Bob Thomas became the starter.

Thomas joked about wearing jersey No. 98 during his football career at Notre Dame between 1971 and 1973. It became problematic, since such a large number typically goes to a huge defensive lineman, not a 5'10" kicker such as Thomas, who weighed just 178 pounds.

"My jersey would always be oversized and I had to cut it down," Thomas said. The worst instance probably was the Orange Bowl game against the University of Nebraska on January 1, 1973, the year before Notre Dame won the national championship. The jersey Thomas received at the Orange Bowl was so big that he could not tuck it into his pants without looking comical.

"I remember going into the training room with this jersey that went down past my knees," Thomas said. "I asked to have it cut," even though it was the only time during his college years that Notre Dame put the names of each player on the back of his jersey.

The request initially surprised those who heard him.

"They said, 'Are you sure you want to cut this? Your name is on the back.' I said, 'If we don't cut it, I'm not going to be able to walk in it, let alone kick in it,'" Thomas recalled.

If worn by a woman, the jersey may have looked like a shapeless, ill-fitting dress. On a football player, the jersey posed another concern.

"I didn't want it to come out of the bottom of my pants," Thomas joked.

Forthright Father

Fr. Riehle and former Notre Dame football coach Bob Davie both laid down roots in Western Pennsylvania before coming to Notre Dame and their common background helped them to establish a bond. The priest's forthrightness, combined with a sense of humor, let him speak frankly about a situation and still draw a laugh.

"He cut right to the core," Davie said. "There was no b.s. with him at all."

After one especially disappointing game, Davie said he turned to Fr. Riehle and was looking for a little sympathy. The coach found none.

When Davie voiced his frustration with the team's performance that day to the chaplain, Fr. Riehle replied, "Yeah, you're right. We were awful."

The priest's bluntness and honesty at that moment caused Davie to laugh, the team's former coach recalled. Fr. Riehle could be counted upon to provide a reality check, along with an unassuming spiritual presence. The coach characterized the clergyman as a "father figure" to everyone.

"He always brought a smile to your face," Davie said. Fr. Riehle could do that even though he never tried to "sugarcoat" anything, the coach added.

Collar-Wearing Cigar Smoker

Sometimes, it was the contrast of Fr. Riehle's cigar-smoking, straight-talking demeanor of a "regular guy" wearing the garb of a priest that turned a situation humorous.

"He used to talk about his finances," Davie said with a chuckle. Fr. Riehle had worked in business, returned to Notre Dame to earn his master's degree in business administration and followed the stock market. The clergyman's business acumen and awareness of the latest financial and economic news seemed a bit of a contradiction for a person who was ordained to help people find the Lord. On the other hand, the priest used his varied interests to connect with people on their own terms.

"I never thought of him as a priest," Davie said. "I was talking to Fr. Riehle as a friend."

Taking a Joke

"I teased him about being in the *Rudy* movie," Davie said about the chaplain. "I would always tease him about, 'Did you get your cut? Did you have to join the Hollywood Actors Guild? Are you still getting royalties from the movie?'"

The chaplain would respond, "I haven't seen anything yet," Davie recalled. "He just enjoyed the back-and-forth and the banter of people."

"The fact that you were the head football coach at Notre Dame was fine but to him it was more about just putting it into perspective," Davie said.

Top 10 Reasons to Confess to Notre Dame's Fr. James Riehle

Confession of one's sins is a key part of the Catholic faith. The following is a Top 10 list of why people may have chosen Fr. Riehle as their confessor.

10. A great choice if you like the smell of cigar smoke.

9. Battle tested by decades of hearing confessions at a college campus.

8. The former hockey player never threw any elbows in a confessional.

7. Find out if he was saving a special penance just for you.

6. Not limited to bankers' hours.

5. Took vows to forgive anything.

4. Football chaplain never gave anyone penance to serve as a tackling dummy.

3. You could open up to Oprah or Dr. Phil, but only Fr. Riehle could grant you absolution.

2. More dignified than baring your soul on *The Jerry Springer Show*.

1. He'd give guidance without handing you a bill.

Chapter 4

PURSUE YOUR MISSION

L ife gains meaning when we are driven by a mission. Fr. Riehle found purpose in his roles as a spiritual leader, an adviser, a friend, a son, a brother and an uncle. Years after his death, Fr. Riehle's influence on those he helped has proven to have lasting value.

"There are many things I remember about playing football at Notre Dame and Fr. Riehle is near the top of that list," said George Hayduk, a defensive lineman for the 1971, 1972 and 1973 Notre Dame football teams.

"I could not go out on the field before the game if I had not knelt before him, and I can still feel his hand on my head as he blessed me," said Hayduk, now retired after working as an account executive for a medical devices company in Scranton, Pennsylvania. "He led us in the Hail Mary before every game and he was as much a part of Notre Dame football as my teammates were and Ara Parseghian. I can still see him standing on the sidelines and at practice with that old cigar."

Fr. Riehle was a "legend at Notre Dame," Holtz said.

"He was there when I got there and he was there when I left," Holtz said. "The athletes confided in him. He was around practice a lot. He was just part of the family."

The team's biggest stars viewed the chaplain as a source of strength and steadiness in a veritable sea of tsunami-like expectations. Those who played infrequently also turned to him. The list of those who credit the chaplain with providing a positive and calming influence include Joe Montana, Joe Theismann, Allen Pinkett, Reggie Brooks and Raghib "Rocket" Ismail. Regardless of their particular faith, they each said the pre-game Mass held by Fr. Riehle during the football season provided a spiritual lift.

"At the team Mass, he always did a good job," Holtz said. "He was always well prepared. He was always very emotional about it. He loved Notre Dame. That came through on a consistent basis. He loved the students. He loved everything about it."

Fr. Riehle's seemingly ubiquitous presence around the university's athletic department facilitated his availability to those who needed his counsel.

"He was very familiar with the kids and the kids would talk to him and open up," said John Whitmer, a retired athletic department trainer. "He was a pretty rational, pretty astute guy."

Counseling Chaplain

David "Kris" Haines, the Notre Dame receiver who caught a touchdown pass from Joe Montana with no time left in the 1979 Cotton Bowl to produce one of the greatest comebacks in Fighting Irish history, said he was among the students who turned to Fr. Riehle for advice. The team chaplain's guidance proved especially useful during the first couple of years that Haines attended the university when his parents were going through a divorce. Such family situations certainly have an unsettling ripple effect on the children, regardless of their age.

"Fr. Riehle was one person I reached out to for guidance," Haines said. "I could trust him. I was sincere with him."

After Haines left Notre Dame, one of his aunts and her husband, the CEO of a company who attended the football team's games regularly, stayed in touch with Fr. Riehle. The aunt, a sister of Haines' father, also converted to Catholicism.

"Fr. Riehle was just so positive and down to Earth," said Haines, who added that the team chaplain encouraged him to develop a prayer life.

"I felt he was one of the big reasons I got through healthy and completed my degree," Haines said about Fr. Riehle.

At the same time, Fr. Riehle's competitive spirit and support for Notre Dame and its athletes was unmistakable.

"He knew football and would get so intense on the sideline," Haines said about Fr. Riehle in his role as the team chaplain.

Similar to many fans, Fr. Riehle reacted with disgust when a critical play or a bad call by the officials at a key point in the contest went against his favorite team.

Crusty Charm

Fr. Riehle's sometimes gruff personality also was accompanied by a crusty charm that allowed people to accept feedback from him that they might reject if it came from anyone else, former football coach Bob Davie said. The clergyman's experience and wisdom gave him gravitas that allowed his views to carry additional weight with people.

"He had a knack for saying things in a non-confrontational way that maybe other people would say and it would be confrontational," Davie said.

Fr. Riehle recognized that people have their strengths and weaknesses.

"You respected what he said because you knew it was the truth," Davie said.

The priest could put situations in their proper perspective and not become "caught up in the hype" of anything, Davie said.

"He got his pleasure out of just interacting with people," Davie said.

Coaches' Confidant

Fr. Riehle's behind-the-scenes work in establishing strong relationships with head coaches and athletic directors who led the university's sports programs was "very important," former Notre Dame President Fr. Edward "Monk" Malloy said. The team chaplain could help to guide them as they tried to navigate their way through the daunting pressures and requirements of their jobs.

Fr. Riehle was a man's man in the "traditional sense of the term," Fr. Malloy said. Without a doubt, the chaplain was "rough and ready," Fr. Malloy added.

Even though Fr. Riehle seemed like a "guy's guy," he certainly was "approachable," former kicker Bob Thomas said.

"He had a gruff way about him but a certain appeal," Thomas said.

"He didn't suffer fools gladly and all of those little expressions," Fr. Malloy said. Fr. Riehle also had "strong opinions" about politics and the church.

"When it came to being there for people when they were sick or when there was a death in the family, or doing weddings or whatever, he was always happy to play the role of priest and pastor," Fr. Malloy said.

Making an Impression

"I got to know Fr. Riehle in the usual way as an undergrad," said John Gaski, now a marketing professor at Notre Dame's business school. "That is, you only get to know him if you get into trouble."

As a Notre Dame undergraduate, various infractions brought Gaski in front of Fr. Riehle during the priest's tenure as dean of students. It was "nothing serious" by today's standards, added Gaski, who received his B.B.A. in 1971 and his M.B.A. in 1973 from Notre Dame.

"I think I probably snuck my car on campus more than anyone in school history," Gaski said. "Why walk when it's 3 a.m. and cold?"

After earning a four-year degree, Gaski ironically returned to Notre Dame as a graduate student and became a resident assistant (R.A.) to help maintain discipline in the dormitory where he was assigned.

Unreceptive Reaction

"During R.A. orientation before the school year, Fr. Riehle was one of the officials to address the group," Gaski said. "You should have seen the glare he gave me when he noticed me in attendance and realized that I was actually going to be an R.A."

The look of incredulity offered the clear impression that Fr. Riehle wondered what would become of the university when someone who had been a disciplinary thorn for the dean of students was becoming a key authority figure in a residence hall.

With Gaski on the faculty, the ranking for Notre Dame's Mendoza College of Business ironically has been on the rise. The business school finished first among undergraduate programs for the fifth year in a row, spanning 2010-2014, in an annual survey of the nation's best business schools by *Bloomberg Businessweek* magazine.

Tumultuous Times

If the best job at Notre Dame was to serve as the football team's chaplain and stand next to the head coach on the 50-yard line, the worst one may have been the role of head of discipline during the volatile Vietnam War era. The latter post was a crucial role that Fr. Riehle performed.

Fr. Riehle had the unenviable duty of keeping the peace during the rebellious period of the late 1960s and early 1970s.

At Notre Dame, upheaval occurred when student protests about the unpopular and ultimately unwinnable Vietnam War left the campus there and at universities elsewhere rife with discord. Violent protests attract headlines but potentially incendiary situations that are defused in time often stay out of the news.

As the dean of students at Notre Dame, he was "fair and honest," retired athletic trainer John Whitmer said.

"But, boy, you didn't want to be summoned to his office," Whitmer emphasized.

Disciplinarian for Disruptive Demonstrators

One of Fr. Riehle's greatest contributions involved serving effectively as Notre Dame's chief disciplinarian during the turbulent time of the Vietnam

War era when student alienation, clashes with administrators and disobedience disrupted the learning atmosphere at college campuses across the country. As other universities turned to the police or the National Guard to safeguard the educational process, Notre Dame President Fr. Theodore Hesburgh called on no-nonsense Fr. Riehle to enforce a rule that proved pivotal in letting students express themselves, within limits.

If campus protests became detrimental to allowing fellow students to attend classes and pursue their education, Fr. Riehle warned them to cease and desist within 15 minutes or face expulsion. Once that so-called "15-minute rule" became university policy, students who tested Fr. Riehle's resolve found that the priest could do more than just talk tough. Due in large part to Fr. Riehle, Notre Dame maintained a learning atmosphere, despite student protests.

"I think a lot of that was a function of the relationship between Fr. Hesburgh and Fr. Riehle," Fr. Malloy said. "They were both on the firing line, in some sense. But they were able to work out a mode of operations that allowed some room for disagreement and yet prevented chaos from getting established."

The "good working relationship" between Fr. Riehle and Fr. Hesburgh "got us through that time," Fr. Malloy said.

Fr. Riehle won praise for handling student protests, with the communication skills he honed as a professional salesman proving valuable during that volatile period.

The innovative 15-minute rule adopted by Fr. Riehle and Fr. Hesburgh to defuse student protests on Notre Dame's campus became a model for other universities to follow. The vast majority of protesting students obeyed the warning, while a small number of those who refused were dismissed from the university and needed to wait to seek readmission.

"It was a most difficult time," former hockey coach Charles "Lefty" Smith said. The Kent State University riots on May 4, 1970, led to a confrontation with Ohio National Guardsmen. At one point, 28 of the 77 guardsmen opened fire in a shooting that left four students dead and nine others wounded. A federal panel, known as the Scranton Commission, investigated the incident and ultimately concluded that the shootings were unjustified.

Five days after the shootings, an estimated 100,000 people descended upon Washington, D.C., to demonstrate against the war and the killing of unarmed Kent State students.

Fr. Riehle did not enjoy the job as the university's chief disciplinarian but he wielded his authority when needed to retain order to preserve the educational process. He may have been ideally suited for that difficult job that could have left a less stouthearted person floundering.

Unenviable Assignment

Fr. Malloy said he was sure that Fr. Riehle was "very happy" when he ultimately finished that assignment.

"He never liked it; that's for sure," Fr. Malloy said about Fr. Riehle's unenviable role as the head of discipline at Notre Dame during the Vietnam War era.

"I think he just felt that out of obedience to duty, that's what he was being called to do and he did it to the best he could," Fr. Malloy said.

Fr. Malloy said his relationship with Fr. Riehle primarily was through their shared allegiance to the university's various sports teams, and as fellow priests and community members at Corby Hall, where campus clergymen work.

"Even though most of us lived in dorms, that [Corby Hall] is our central operating place," Fr. Malloy said. "We have meals there and we have a chapel there."

Managed an Impossible Task

Fr. Riehle's "uniquely masculine yet tender persona" marked his tenure as dean of students, as Pangborn Hall rector, as the Monogram Club's executive director and as athletic chaplain presiding at the Notre Dame football team's game-day Mass, recalled Gary Caruso, a 1973 Notre Dame graduate.

Caruso, who became a Washington-based communications strategist and a legislative and public affairs director in President Bill Clinton's administration, said Fr. Riehle "successfully managed an impossible task," while serving as dean of students during the height of the Vietnam War.

Fr. Riehle was the rules-enforcing authority on the Notre Dame campus, which Caruso described as an insulated Catholic educational enclave. However, Notre Dame students at that time knew roommates, classmates, friends or family members who served in Vietnam and, in too many instances, lost their lives in the defense of freedom.

"The harsh reality became starkly visual one day when someone planted more than 200 white crosses on the South Quad, each representing a lost Notre Dame graduate," Caruso wrote in a guest editorial in the February 19, 2009, issue of the *Observer*, the campus newspaper.

Even after two strokes forced Fr. Riehle to start using a golf cart to travel on campus once a cane no longer was sufficient, the increasingly frail man never lost his measured temperament, his sense of justice or his legendary wit, Caruso said.

"As dean of students, Riehle ruled autonomously in a time that university President Emeritus Fr. Theodore Hesburgh calls the student 'revolution,'" Caruso said.

Indelible Images

The 1970 Notre Dame yearbook, *Dome,* includes a photograph on page 336 of Fr. Riehle in the Main Building looking at his watch to time a warning to more than 100 students protesting on-campus recruiting by the Central Intelligence Agency and Dow Chemical, which manufactured napalm, Caruso pointed out.

Enforcement of the 15-minute rule was no idle threat to those who refused to cease and desist that day. Fr. Riehle expelled five students and suspended five others but all of them, except one, chose to return and to earn a degree.

A photograph of Fr. Riehle on page 280 of the 1976 Notre Dame student yearbook exhibits the highly sociable side of the priest, who even at a time of turmoil "mingled with students and shared mutual respect," Caruso wrote in the *Observer*.

"The photograph shows Riehle at the Senior Bar with his signature cigar in hand while grasping a plastic cup of beer and speaking with a student who held a beer as well," Caruso wrote. "It reveals how Riehle lived a measured Sheriff Andy Taylor existence during the height of the Vietnam War's upheaval years."

The fictional Sheriff Andy Taylor, of *The Andy Griffith Show* from 1960 to 1968, devoted a good deal of his time to philosophizing with and calming down the people portrayed in the small town of Mayberry, North Carolina, much as Fr. Riehle did with the students at Notre Dame. When Sheriff Taylor needed to put someone in jail, he did so, but with the intent of rehabilitating the person by talking about the unlawful behavior and the need to reform.

Repentance Requested

During Fr. Riehle's tenure as dean of students, Caruso recalled installing a 10-button telephone as a switchboard for rooms in a Lyons Hall wing. It may have been an enterprising use of the latest technology at the time but Caruso had not received permission to do so.

"The phone company removed it and notified Riehle," Caruso said.

"On days when I had a class in the administration building, I would pop my head into the Dean of Students' office on the third floor to say hello or check on projects I was working on for student government," Caruso said. "Since my student government days ended with the start of my senior year, my visits with Fr. Riehle were only social affairs. About a month into my first semester of senior year, I was chatting with Fr. Riehle, when he said, almost in passing, 'Oh, I was going to call you. I received a report from the phone company that said you had a 10-button phone in your room. They came out to check a short in the system. Did you steal that?'"

"Yes," Caruso said he answered.

"'Well, the phone company took the phone,'" Fr. Riehle replied and then paused for a moment to scan a report on his desk before continuing, "'and does not recommend anything. So don't do that again.'"

For Caruso, Fr. Riehle's form of discipline was akin to the Lenten season for Catholics who are urged to put sinful ways aside and consider observing increased penance, charity and service to others during the weeks between Ash Wednesday and Easter. The hope is that such behaviors will become the norm after Lent, much the way Fr. Riehle tried to prepare Notre Dame students to live good and meaningful lives after they left the university, as well as during the time they were in school.

As each year ushers in the season of Lent, Caruso said he is reminded of Fr. Riehle's often pronounced verdict and signature comment, "Don't do that again."

Maverick Marine

Mike Whalen, a former Marine, CBS Sports producer and New York-born Republican, has met presidents, popes, members of England's royal family, men who have walked on the moon, Medal of Honor awardees, Heisman Trophy winners and Olympians.

"I have known some great people and I'd consider Fr. Riehle one of them," Whalen said "He was a great guy."

Fr. Riehle also was the key person at Notre Dame who helped Whalen to avoid expulsion from the university. Whalen, partly due to his service in the Marine Corps, had endured unfortunate life experiences at a young age that many of his classmates only could imagine. Those experiences also caused him to struggle in accepting and in adhering to the rigid behavioral rules that Notre Dame had in place at the time.

"I had a girlfriend and she had spent a lot of time in my room with me," said Whalen, who acknowledged having a chronic problem with the university's strict rules that limited the circumstances and the specific times females could visit an all-male residence hall.

"Fr. Riehle had already seen me a bunch of times," Whalen said.

When a Notre Dame dean wanted to expel Whalen from the university, Fr. Riehle held the position of dean of students and faced extreme pressure from the administrator to oust the former Marine.

Whalen's Wait

Whalen recalled sitting outside of Fr. Riehle's office as the dean could be heard raising his voice on the other side of the wall to urge the priest to dismiss the student from Notre Dame.

"I'm sitting there thinking my goose is probably cooked," Whalen said.

Fr. Riehle, well acquainted with Whalen from summoning him many times to his office for one infraction or another, also knew that Whalen's father, an investment banker who helped the Vatican with its investments years before a scandal caused huge losses, had died of a heart attack during June of the student's freshman year. Since Fr. Riehle's dad also had died of a heart attack during the winter of his freshman year at Notre Dame, the priest could appreciate Whalen's independent streak that the sudden loss of a parent could force a young person to develop quickly out of necessity.

Whalen also said he had been a "wannabe" hockey player who shared Fr. Riehle's love of the sport. In addition, they both had served their country in the military, so Fr. Riehle raised no eyebrows if the student used salty language when they talked, Whalen said. Fr. Riehle simply applied his knack of knowing how to communicate with people of various backgrounds in a way that made each feel comfortable.

When the dean left Fr. Riehle's office, the administrator had a brief but testy conversation with Whalen about his likely involuntary departure from Notre Dame in the coming minutes.

Once Whalen entered Fr. Riehle's office and sat down, the priest minced no words in between puffs of his seemingly ever-present cigar. Fr. Riehle confirmed that the College of Arts and Letters' Associate Dean Devere Plunkett, A.M., wanted to boot the student's "ass" out of Notre Dame, Whalen recalled.

"Devere Plunkett wants you expelled; I'm probably going to have to suspend you," Whalen recalled Fr. Riehle saying.

Ground Support

Suddenly, two other university officials who had learned of the critical meeting about the student's tenuous future at the university contacted Fr. Riehle to voice support for Whalen.

First, Fr. Riehle's phone rang and the head of the university's business school was calling to speak on Whalen's behalf, the student recalled. Second, Leo Corbaci, the university's registrar, came into Fr. Riehle's office and sat down to back the student.

Whalen's latest bout of trouble stemmed from the entrepreneurial way he found to earn about $10,000 a semester while attending school full-time. He had learned how to help his fellow classmates gain access to the courses they wanted to take by obtaining IBM computer punch cards from other students during the course registration process, duplicating the cards in the basement of the university's computer center and selling each duplicate for $20 or $25.

During course registration, a student collected a punch card for each course that he wanted to take. The student then was supposed to submit all of the cards at the end of the process to enroll in courses for that semester.

Whalen would ask his friends to pick up computer punch cards for courses that he knew others wanted but may not have had sufficient seniority to gain a slot before the openings were filled. In such instances, he asked for the cards to be given to him to duplicate. Those who ever attended a university and found themselves unable to sign up for a course he or she really needed or wanted to take can appreciate the value of such a service.

The students who bought the duplicate punch cards then could gain a spot in a course that otherwise might have been closed to them if others had filled the openings first. Whalen said he could overbook courses by about 10-15 percent, similar to the way airlines might sell extra tickets due to the expectation of certain passengers canceling or changing their plans. But he tried to limit the number of computer punch cards he sold for each course to avoid causing big problems. He learned his lesson about overbooking after selling too many punch cards to one course and creating a severe overcrowding problem. Whalen said he exercised care in future semesters to guard against a recurrence.

Computer-Card Complications

Money earned from the venture went to help his then-widowed mother, his grandmother and his sister, said Whalen, who added he used student loans and worked at four different part-time jobs to pay his way through Notre Dame after the death of his dad. But at the time he was in Fr. Riehle's office to face judgment, the priority for the senior was not to sustain his money-making venture but to proceed toward graduation unimpeded.

Whalen said he had been careful only to transact business with students who he knew and trusted to keep his entrepreneurial activity confidential. However, someone Whalen knew asked him to help a student who was outside of his social circle. The latter student ended up in trouble with university officials and sought leniency in his punishment by offering to disclose how fellow students had been able to buy punch cards to register for courses that otherwise would be have closed to them, Whalen recalled. That student fingered Whalen.

Now on the verge of expulsion, with an influential dean openly seeking the student's ouster from the university, Whalen proposed a way for each side to move forward.

What a Deal!

"Let's make a deal," Whalen, a senior business student, proposed to Fr. Riehle. The student used the same words as the title of a popular daytime television game show, *Let's Make a Deal*, which aired between 1963 and 1977 and featured affable host Monty Hall.

Fr. Riehle inquired about the specifics of the deal.

Since Whalen had amassed enough credits to graduate at the end of that semester, the embattled student offered to tell how he was able to help his fellow students register for coveted courses and how university officials could stop the unorthodox practice from recurring. In exchange, Whalen wanted to be allowed to graduate and avoid any further repercussions regarding his entrepreneurial venture.

Fr. Riehle paused to light a new cigar. Moments later, he accepted the deal. The priest and the registrar then learned that the preventive measure to stop the practice of duplicating the punch cards simply required putting a punch hole in one column on the edge of each card, Whalen said.

"I graduated one semester early in December of 1973," Whalen said. "One of the first persons to congratulate me was Fr. Riehle."

Whalen said he recalled Fr. Riehle telling him, "I can't believe you're getting out of here with a diploma."

Vietnam Fallout

The Vietnam War altered the lives of the roughly 2,700,000 American men and women who served there. Sadly, the Vietnam War caused the death of more than 3 million people, including 58,000 Americans, according to the U.S. Veterans Administration (VA).

The withdrawal of U.S. ground troops from Vietnam in March 1973 simply ended the continuation of U.S. casualties but the fallout from the war that began with the early deployment of troops until the pullout left many veterans who survived the conflict suffering from adverse health effects. The problems included contact with Agent Orange, as well as readjustment.

But many of those physical problems surfaced years after service, while the mental stress on veterans was immediate. The stress easily could be exacerbated by returning home to face personal criticism or worse from many of their fellow countrymen who opposed the war. The hostile reception for numerous Vietnam veterans magnified the stress of their combat experiences, according to the VA.

Fr. Riehle needed to help returning Vietnam veterans try to readjust to campus life. He displayed a fatherly understanding when they encountered problems at school that may well have stemmed from post-traumatic stress, Whalen said.

Theology Throw-Down

In a required theology course at Notre Dame, Whalen said he witnessed a young, anti-war priest chastise a student who had served in Vietnam for an incident that involved the shooting of a five-year-old boy. The priest took the position that the veteran had killed the child without sufficient justification, even though Whalen said enemy forces in South Vietnam reportedly had given the boy a hand grenade and instructed him to use it against the American troops. When the boy pulled the pin of the grenade, Whalen said his classmate needed to shoot the boy before he could toss it at the American soldiers.

Unfortunately, the besieged classmate also exhibited a "1,000-yard stare," a vacant expression shown by many soldiers who had been involved in combat, Whalen said. Such soldiers seemed to focus on a far-away object or appear unresponsive to external stimuli.

Rather than turn the discussion toward the horrors of war and the difficulties faced by everyone from civilians to soldiers, the instructor unrelentingly criticized the student who had served in the Army, Whalen said. Tensions escalated until the student, who appeared to Whalen to be suffering from post-traumatic stress disorder, left the classroom to defuse the incendiary debate.

Still not content, the instructor interjected one last verbal dig at the student who just departed and told the class that they just observed a so-called American war hero who had shot a kid, Whalen said. The former Marine said he had heard enough of the verbal bashing of his fellow veteran from someone who seemed to fit the stereotype of an academician cut off from the boots-on-the-ground reality of a soldier who faced both conventional and unconventional threats.

Classroom Cursing

"F_ck you, Father," Whalen recalled saying, just before he punctuated his declaration by kicking out a classroom window.

"It cost me $900," Whalen said.

Although Whalen's contribution to the class discussion lacked eloquence, it was filled with the conviction of someone who had served his country in an unpopular war and returned to a mixed reception back home. Whalen was one of many students who Fr. Riehle tried to help readjust to campus life after military service.

That time period brewed rebellion of one kind or another when it appeared that the social fabric of society was unraveling. The expanded use of illegal drugs such as heroin and LSD, a sexual revolution, women's liberation, the burning of draft cards, the hippy movement and clandestine resistance to civil rights advances complicated the challenge of university administrators and law enforcement throughout the country.

Smoke Signals

Whalen, now a military contractor who also organizes trips by prominent football coaches and other distinguished Americans to visit troops overseas, said he stayed in touch with Fr. Riehle after graduation. Fr. Riehle occasionally would send notes in the mail to Whalen, who would return to the campus once in a while to smoke cigars with Fr. Riehle, take him out for a meal to Barnaby's Restaurant or go to another favorite haunt. The pair also sometimes smoked cigars with Fr. Hesburgh, who had been the university's president when Whalen was a student.

"I smoked cigars with Fr. Hesburgh in his office," Whalen said about his post-graduation visits.

One time, Whalen recalled meeting with Fr. Riehle in Rome. Whalen was there visiting Cardinals who worked in the Vatican, while Fr. Riehle was accompanying a Notre Dame tour group.

For someone who needed to discipline students, Fr. Riehle somehow managed to retain a rapport with many of them that continued long after they left Notre Dame.

Apt Advice

Fr. Riehle's message to those who he advised often was simple but clear.

"I always remember Fr. Riehle telling me to be happy," Whalen said.

Life unquestionably has its problems but its blessings, too. Days of disappointment happen to everyone. The opportunity is the response. Optimism trumps pessimism. Hope beats despair. A great attitude tops complaining.

"So many people are unhappy all the time and I feel sorry for them," Whalen said.

According to Ephesians 5, "You were once in darkness, but now you are in light in the Lord. Live as children of light, for light produces every kind of goodness and righteousness and truth. Try to learn what is pleasing to the Lord. Take no part in the fruitless works of darkness…"

'Super Sensitive'

When Fr. Riehle served as dean of students, he dutifully enforced Notre Dame's strict student rules and punished offenders. Frankly, anyone who holds the job of campus disciplinarian has a thankless task. Fr. Riehle performed the role without taking pleasure from it. Although he looked and acted the part of a tough guy who students knew could expel, suspend or otherwise sanction them, his former secretary Marge Stranz said Fr. Riehle actually was a "super sensitive" person. She recalled occasionally seeing him shed tears before or after meeting with a student who he needed to penalize.

"I think it was very difficult at times for him," said Stranz, who served as Fr. Riehle's secretary during his entire tenure as dean of students.

Despite his "tender-hearted" tendencies, Fr. Riehle handled discipline "very well," Stranz said.

"The rules were the rules and he had to enforce them," Stranz said.

'Fear' Factor

Due to the nature of the job, anyone who served as Notre Dame's dean of students triggered trepidation among those summoned to appear before him.

"When students came in, they were terrified," Stranz said. The person who held the job at a given time really did not matter, as far as assuaging a sense of foreboding felt by students ordered to appear for judgment about an infraction.

"Everybody was terrified when they got the summons in the form of a post card to see the dean of students," Stranz said. "The disciplinary code then was very strict."

Everything seemingly was against the rules, Stranz said. The voluminous rules written in the student handbook contained plenty of ways for violations to incur, even for the well-intentioned.

College behavior that is considered normal now broke the student-handbook rules when Fr. Riehle needed to mete out punishment. Violations involved drinking alcohol, missing curfew and bringing a car onto campus.

Curfew would be violated if a student failed to return to his dormitory for the night by a specified time. If a student signed in at his residence hall late, even by just minutes, the normal penalty would be a ban on leaving the campus for at least two weeks. The penalty would increase by another two weeks for every additional 15-minute increment of tardiness, Stranz recalled.

During Fr. Riehle's tenure, freshmen were ineligible to bring cars onto campus and sophomores only gained the right in the early 1970s. Initially, only seniors could keep cars on campus. Juniors later gained the privilege. But freshmen needed to focus on acclimating to life at an academically demanding university without the distractions that a car could cause. Nor could underclassmen live off campus.

Monday Morning's Mail

Students on campus who enjoyed their weekends a little too much at Notre Dame sometimes needed to see the dean of students to explain their behavior. A list of infractions from the previous weekend would be passed along to the office of the dean of students on Monday morning and Stranz would schedule each student who was accused to appear for a half-hour meeting. She tried to spread the number of cases throughout each week that the office was open.

"On Monday, I had tons of stuff to do," Stranz said.

Although she allocated 30 minutes to let Fr. Riehle adjudicate each matter, Stranz said he did not spend "tons of time" on disciplinary cases.

Part of the reason involved previously established penalties for each type of infraction. For example, a second instance of academic dishonesty for a student would result in dismissal from the university, Stranz said. Such students would have squandered their second chance.

One aspect of Fr. Riehle's role as dean of students that most people may not have known about was that he spent a good deal of time counseling those who came before him and assisting them in regaining any privileges that an infraction may have forced him to take away temporarily.

Fr. Riehle helped a number of students "straighten out," after they engaged in unacceptable behavior, Stranz said.

"He tried to help you work through it," Stranz said. "If you were suspended or expelled, he would try to help you. He basically was a very kind person."

Fr. Riehle also communicated well with her, Stranz said.

"We did talk a lot," Stranz said. "My office was on one side of the hall and his office was across the hall. The main office was right next to us. He would come over to talk."

'Black Mc'

The most feared campus disciplinarian, in Stranz's recollection, was not Fr. Riehle but one of his predecessors from the 1950s, Fr. Charles McCarragher, who the students nicknamed "Black Mc" for the black cassock that he always wore.

"I worked in the discipline office before Fr. Riehle," Stranz said. "Fr. McCarragher was feared; Oh, my!"

Stranz described Fr. McCarragher as a "tough man."

Everybody who followed in that role always was feared, Stranz said.

Fr. McCarragher served as "prefect of students" before he left the job in 1957 to become vice president of student affairs and built a reputation as the "favorite target for any and all complaints about the university," according to Notre Dame's 1968 student yearbook.

During a 49-year career at Notre Dame that began when she was just 16 and ended with her retirement, Stranz said that Fr. Riehle and another former dean of students, Fr. A. Leonard Collins, who succeeded Fr. McCarragher in that job during the fall of 1957, rank among her "very favorite" bosses.

Aside from Fr. Riehle's sense of humor, his likable nature led him to receive many social invitations and he tried to extend the hospitality to others when he had the chance.

Stranz said the most fun she had with Fr. Riehle occurred after he introduced her to one of his friends who was "very wealthy" and had married a business woman from Chicago. The couple had a place on a lake and invited a number of Notre Dame priests and university employees who otherwise could not have enjoyed such surroundings to spend the day there and to stay for dinner.

"We did that several times a summer," Stranz said.

Sports Chaplain

One of the best transitions in Fr. Riehle's life likely occurred when he fulfilled his duties as dean of students and gained a new assignment as Notre Dame's head sports chaplain.

Fr. Riehle "really found his niche" when he went to the athletic department, Stranz said.

Coaches, players and trainers said they enjoyed him serving as their chaplain, too. He left what he referred to as the worst job on campus for what many observers would describe as one of the best.

Travel Team

Fr. Malloy, a professor of theology at Notre Dame, served as the university's 16th president between 1987 and 2005 when Fr. Riehle was the athletics department chaplain and executive director of the Monogram Club.

"I would always be invited to go to major events with the Monogram Club," Fr. Malloy said.

Fr. Malloy recalled accepting invitations from Fr. Riehle to concelebrate Masses, as well as to give talks at athletic department and Monogram Club activities.

Periodically, Fr. Malloy would accompany Fr. Riehle and the football team on road trips, including bowl games. They also sometimes traveled together with the basketball team. Fittingly, Fr. Malloy was a standout basketball player at Archbishop Carroll High School in Washington, D.C. His teammates included John Thompson, an ESPN talk show host who coached the Georgetown University basketball team to a 1984 national championship.

Bus 4 Bonding

One particularly vivid memory that Fr. Malloy had of Fr. Riehle was the chaplain riding to and from airports and games on "Bus 4" with the coaches, sports trainers, physicians and support staffers who traveled with the team. Fr. Riehle, the physicians and usually a few other people would "hang out in the back," Fr. Malloy said. They were "delighted" when the team won and "depressed" when it lost, he added.

As a result, Fr. Riehle developed a "very close working relationship" with many of the non-students who were connected to the football program, Fr. Malloy said.

"He had a special role, I think, in the lives of a lot of people that were behind the scenes of the football program," Fr. Malloy said.

Relaxing with the Reverend

Athletic team support staffers and Fr. Riehle could relax a little when they boarded Bus 4.

"It was all adults," Whitmer said. "He could kind of let his hair down and just be a regular guy."

Since Fr. Riehle worked and lived in the "real world" after graduating from Notre Dame in 1949 and did not enter the seminary until the late 1950s, he was a "unique individual," Whitmer said.

"By having that experience, it made him a very good, sound adviser," Whitmer said.

Bus 4 became a haven for a great deal of conversation and "good fellowship," particularly if Notre Dame had won the game.

Pastoral Presence

Notre Dame coaches worked under immense pressure and relied on Fr. Riehle to help them persevere amid the lofty expectations of alumni and a devoted national fan base.

"That was his duty and he loved it," said Marty Gleason, a former president of the Notre Dame Club of Chicago, whose father's older brother was a classmate of "Rudy" Ruettiger's father in high school where they grew up in Joliet, Illinois.

As stress mounted, coaches and players turned to Fr. Riehle for wise counsel.

"The coaching staff just loved Jim Riehle and the teams did, as well," Gleason said.

The chaplain also was a guiding influence for many players during their Notre Dame years and a personal connection with the university when they left school.

"He was able to establish incredible relationships when players would graduate," Gleason said.

Thanksgiving Tales

Fr. Riehle's nephew Jim Ruse said his uncle "definitely" was a "hero" to him. The talents that the nephew and his sister, Deirdre, noticed in their uncle may not be what others would necessarily expect.

One example was their uncle's mastery of piling an impressive amount of food onto a single plate. Years of attending banquets and fundraisers that involved navigating buffet lines gave Fr. Riehle a well-honed skill set that caused his nephew and niece to marvel at their uncle's creativity in maximizing the amount of food that could be placed in a very limited amount of space.

"He wasn't a big man by any stretch physically but he could definitely fill his plate at Thanksgiving," his nephew said. "My sister and I would just always laugh hysterically at looking at his Thanksgiving plate. It was just this heaping mass of everything he could possibly stuff on there."

It was amazing to see Fr. Riehle eat the huge mound of whatever he put on his plate, let alone watch him head back for even more helpings of the Thanksgiving feast, his nephew said.

'Super-Choice' Seats

Family members who gave Fr. Riehle advance notice could obtain "super-choice" seats for home football games by reimbursing the chaplain for the expense of the tickets. After all, the team chaplain had an enviable place to stand on the sidelines and did not need to use the seats himself.

Jim Ruse said he attended an average of two or three Notre Dame football games a year with his parents.

As a boy, Notre Dame was the nephew's favorite team and he recalls always pestering his uncle to take him into the locker room. One Saturday, the boy's dream came true.

Near the end of the 1973 national championship season, Fr. Riehle took his nephew Jim into the team's locker room. In his characteristic gruffness, Fr. Riehle then told his nephew to take his program from that day's Notre Dame-Air Force football game and seek out the players for autographs.

"I turned around and kind of looked in the locker room and went, "Uh-oh! I don't know who any of these people are. They don't have their jerseys on anymore," the nephew said with a hearty laugh. "So, that was a little tough for me being about in the fifth grade or right about in there."

Notre Dame's kicker at the time was Bob Thomas, an Academic All-American who later had a successful, 12-year playing career in the National Football League that included 10 years with the Chicago Bears. Thomas ultimately became a justice of the Illinois Supreme Court. But on the day Fr. Riehle's nephew needed a guide in the Notre Dame locker room, Thomas came to the rescue by introducing the lad to various players to obtain their autographs. It also must have been pretty cool to have been befriended by Thomas, who in his final Notre Dame game kicked a 19-yard field goal against the University of Alabama at the 1973 Sugar Bowl in New Orleans late in the game to give the Fighting Irish a 24-23 victory and the national title.

"I got a whole bunch of autographs," recalled the nephew, whose voice still conveyed excitement more than four decades later. "It was probably one of the highlights of my life."

As a youngster, the nephew enjoyed tracking the kicker's career as he ended up playing for Ruse's favorite professional team, the Chicago Bears.

Basketball Bonus

"When walking back to Pangborn Hall with my father and Uncle Jim after that football game with my autographed program in hand, my uncle pointed out a small group of very tall black men and said to me, 'Go ask those guys for their autographs,'" Jim Ruse recalled. "I remember being nervous, but did as he instructed. Those five guys were so nice to me and opened my football program and each signed it."

Only when checking the program more than 40 years later to gather information to include in this book did Jim Ruse realize that those tall Notre Dame students were basketball players.

"And, just now, today, I realized that those five signatures are from Gary Brokaw, Ray Martin, John Shumate, Dwight Clay and Adrian Dantley," Jim Ruse said. "Hmmmm, wasn't that the starting line-up of the ND team that famously-beat UCLA during the '73-'74 season ending that long UCLA unbeaten streak? I guess my uncle must have received a tip from God in advance... LOL. How's that for weird??? Wow! I might have to put this program in the security deposit box at the bank."

That historic game marked a battle of unbeaten teams, No. 1-ranked UCLA and No. 2-rated Notre Dame. The game featured a combined eight participants from both sides who later played in the National Basketball Association (NBA). The Fighting Irish came storming back at home to win, 72-71, by scoring the final 12 points of the contest in an astounding late-game run against a UCLA team coached by the legendary John Wooden, led by star center Bill Walton and infused with confidence stemming from its string of 88 wins. The victory on January 19, 1974, followed just 19 days after Thomas booted his 19-yard field goal to win the national championship for the Notre Dame football team.

Old-School Uncle

Fr. Riehle might best be characterized as an "old-school man's man," said his nephew Jim Ruse. "But that didn't mean he didn't appreciate what anybody was or whatever they did. That was cool with him. You wouldn't think of him being a priest. If you meet a hundred priests in your life, with 90 of them you could say, 'Yeah, that guy's a priest.' But not my uncle, he wasn't like that at all."

However, when people needed a good listener and a trustworthy confidant, Fr. Riehle was a straightforward source of wisdom and understanding. In that sense, he was as priestly as anyone.

"I think he started being a priest in his late 30s or early 40s, so he had already gone through a good portion of his life, as opposed to many people who go through the seminary being very young," his nephew said. "While he was kind of gruff and rough about things, he knew when to shut up and listen and offer the right advice."

Even though Jim Ruse viewed his Uncle Jim as a hero, the admiration did not mean the nephew or other children in the family never irritated their esteemed relative.

"He was a typical uncle who didn't have kids," Ruse said with amusement. "When he had enough of me or my sister or any of my cousins, he'd get pissed."

The opportunity to leave the presence of riled up nephews or nieces always was an option for Fr. Riehle. That same freedom is not possessed by parents who need to endure the mood swings of children without escape.

Understood Aspiring Athletes

"He was kind of a rough guy and a good athlete," Jim Ruse said about his uncle. "He was always kind of ribbing you and trying to make you a little tougher."

Fr. Riehle was a practitioner of "reverse psychology" with his verbal barbs, his nephew recalled. The priest's comments may have seemed aimed at questioning someone's skill to achieve a goal but the real intent was to spur someone to heightened accomplishments.

"If I was out in the driveway playing basketball while I was in grade school and I bragged that I could make whatever shot, he just basically wouldn't even say anything," Jim Ruse recalled. "He'd have a cigar hanging out of his mouth and just kind of laughed like he's not going to pay any attention to me, so I took it as a challenge. If I made the shot, he would just sort of keep walking and laugh."

The follow-up laugh was about as close to him saying "good boy" in response to his nephew backing up his boasts but his approval was conveyed nonetheless with non-verbal signals.

"That was about all you got out of him either way," Jim Ruse recalled.

Competitive Chaplain

No one should have underestimated the competitive streak of the Notre Dame chaplain, who proved to be adept at a variety of sports. He also sometimes challenged his fellow competitors to make plays that seemed too difficult to achieve. When his nephew was in junior high school, his uncle told the boy that there was "no way" the youngster could sink a 30-foot chip shot from off of the green.

"I put it in, and I'm not a good golfer by any stretch, especially the way he played," Jim Ruse said. "He was just almost fit to be tied that I made the thing."

Despite his uncle's disbelieving gestures and comments, it was clear to his nephew that the animated actions hid a sense of satisfaction at seeing the accomplishment.

"He always had that sly grin, with a cigar hanging out of his mouth, and you knew he was proud of you – even though he was pissed," Jim Ruse said with a hearty laugh.

World's Best Job?

What better job in the world could anybody have who loved God and sports than to be the athletic chaplain at a place such as Notre Dame? His nephew said the job fit his uncle and his interests perfectly.

"He was kind of quiet and stoic," Jim Ruse said. There were times when the nephew recalled becoming a little frightened as a boy when his uncle's ire was raised about something.

At the same time, the uncle also could be surprisingly funny, his nephew said.

20-Minute Masses

During his visits to see family, Fr. Riehle sometimes celebrated his quick Masses that helped to boost his popularity with time-pressured Notre Dames students.

"It was neat having Communion at the house when he'd come and visit," Jim Ruse said. "He did his trademark 20-minute Mass and we were out the door. As kids, that was great."

Several years ago, Jim Ruse said a customer entered his audio-visual services retail store in downtown Homewood, Illinois, and she mentioned that she knew Fr. Riehle. When the patron was told that the priest was the store owner's uncle, she recounted attending and enjoying his Masses as a Notre Dame student.

"We used to make sure we always got up on time on Sunday to go to his Mass," the former student said.

"I started laughing," said Jim Ruse, whose former store called "Rooster" provided audio-visual equipment rental, as well as production services for corporations and small-budget videos. "I told her the reason she liked it so much was that the Masses were only 20 minutes long."

She confessed appreciating that Mass attendance could be condensed into such a short time period to let her do other things for the rest of the day, he remembered.

"He had a bit of a reputation for getting to the point," said Jim Ruse, who added that his uncle did not mince words about anything. The priest did what he needed to do expeditiously.

Conservative Political Leanings

"He was definitely a conservative Republican," Jim Ruse said about his uncle. "Up until the very end, I was driving back and forth with my father when he [Uncle Jim] would have parts of his legs amputated because of diabetes. I would even rib him a little bit about, 'You're going for Obama' or 'You're going for Hillary' or whoever."

Fr. Riehle would just "grunt" his disdain for liberal politicians, his nephew said. His uncle favored successful businessman and former Massachusetts Gov. Mitt Romney, who lost the Republican presidential nomination in 2008 to Sen. John McCain and the presidential election in 2012 to incumbent President Obama.

As conservative as Fr. Riehle was in his political views, he was open-minded and did not try to "push" his religious beliefs on anybody, his nephew said.

"I thought it was very admirable just to let people be who they are but to make sure that you had certain things in your life that counted," Jim Ruse said. As a former salesman, Fr. Riehle learned when he was on the road about "when to shut up" and let someone else talk, his nephew said.

"I think he was really good at that," his nephew said.

Sly Smile

A sly smile was a near constant with the priest, regardless of the topic at a given time.

That smile almost was always there, whether he was "pissed off" or he thought something was funny, his nephew recalled.

His uncle also became known toward the end of his life when he disagreed with people for saying, "You don't know what you're talking about."

Although that comment typically cut off a conversation and sometimes annoyed those who were the recipients of the retort, it was apparent that the verbal exchange was "all in fun," the nephew said with a laugh.

"It was just time to move on with the next conversation," his nephew said.

It would have been interesting to have known Fr. Riehle when he was in high school as he pursued his passions in sports and acting, his nephew said. The uncle had performed in plays in his youth. His nephew said he did not know about it until after his uncle's funeral. His Uncle Jim seldom talked about himself.

It was "really cool" that his uncle was able to relate with people in a direct and fundamental way that still respected those he met, Jim Ruse said. That trait might explain why many people "drove for hours" to attend his funeral and pay their respects, his nephew said.

"It was amazing," Jim Ruse said.

Reflexive Reactions

"My uncle didn't have the biggest fondness for cats," the nephew said.

During one visit, Fr. Riehle's sister put her cat in the basement while the family sat down for a meal. As the cat became frisky, it began to scratch at the basement door and bump up against it to protest the restrictions that had been placed on it. It was funny to watch his uncle's reaction to the mysterious noises that were coming from the nearby door, since the cause of the commotion was not visible, his nephew recalled.

Another time, Fr. Riehle and his brother-in-law became stuck together in a sliding glass door. Both men had gone outdoors to watch a storm develop in the darkening sky. Suddenly, thunder and lightning struck violently.

Startled, the two "chunky men" bolted back toward the house, Jim Ruse recalled. As they tried to race inside, they inadvertently became wedged together trying to squeeze through an opening in the sliding glass door.

"They both entered the door at the same time, so they got stuck in the door jam," the nephew said with amusement. As a boy witnessing the event, it was "pretty funny," he recalled.

"I still can see it happening and laughing my butt off," the nephew said.

Chapter 5

FIND FULFILLMENT BY HELPING OTHERS

F r. Riehle's dedication to Notre Dame students and graduates was "embodied" in a television advertisement in which the priest was shown walking across campus with former quarterback Joe Montana and facetiously asking the then-NFL star what he had done since leaving there. The question was posed in a humorous vein but still reflected the kind of interest that Fr. Riehle took in people, who he encouraged to do their best, said Allen Pinkett, a former Fighting Irish running back and the on-air analyst for the football team's radio broadcasts.

"His presence made you act more responsibly, not because he had a big brother effect, but because you wanted to make him proud," Pinkett said.

One year when the Notre Dame football team was heading to the Fiesta Bowl, Marty Gleason, a former president of the Notre Dame Club of Chicago, had trouble obtaining a commercial flight that would allow him to return after the football game in Arizona for a business meeting in the Midwest the following day. He mentioned his dilemma to Fr. Riehle, who arranged for Gleason to obtain a seat on a chartered plane that already had been lined up for others to fly to the game and return shortly thereafter.

Not wanting to miss the chartered flight from South Bend, Gleason also obtained Fr. Riehle's assistance to stay at the Ivy Court Inn, where the football team typically spent the night before each game. The overnight stay allowed Gleason to avoid potential weather problems that could have delayed his arrival from Chicago and assure that he could make the departing flight.

Friend's Funeral Mass

Daniel Gibbs Jr., a former president of the Notre Dame Club of Chicago who preceded Gleason in the role, battled cancer before the disease claimed his life. Fr. Riehle provided spiritual guidance through the periods of diagnosis, the treatment and just prior to the club leader's death.

"Dan was a close friend of Fr. Riehle," Gleason said.

Fr. Riehle presided at Dan's funeral Mass and, as usual, found the right words to share with the family and friends who gathered.

"Dan's wife and children still have a very high regard for Jim Riehle," Gleason said.

People gravitated toward the priest, who seemed happy to be of service.

"They always felt very comfortable with Jim Riehle," Gleason said.

Team-only Mass

For a special wedding anniversary, the parents of a friend of Gleason received an invitation from Fr. Riehle to attend a team-only pre-game Mass. The Mass was held at Moreau Seminary before a home football game and it was an experience that the couple truly enjoyed, Gleason said.

"Fr. Riehle was very respectful of people's parents," Gleason explained. Fr. Riehle may have been especially sensitive about such situations because of the premature death of his own father during the future priest's freshman year at Notre Dame. The chaplain seemed highly solicitous about honoring special requests for parents.

"All of the players attended the Mass," Gleason said. "It was a serious ceremony."

Prayers would be said during the Mass to ask God to protect the players from injuries. As usual, Fr. Riehle kept the Mass short.

"But he always made his point," whenever it came time to deliver a homily to put the readings of the Mass in perspective, Gleason said.

Scholarship Fund

The Brennan-Boland-Riehle Scholarship Fund provides need-based financial aid to Notre Dame students who are children of dues-paying members of the university's Monogram Club, which consists of past winners of athletic letters. Two funds merged in 1979 under the names of Brennan and Boland. The fund's third name, Riehle, was added in June of 2004. The fund honors: Joe Boland, a Rockne-era football player who served as an Irish assistant coach, alumni director and football radio voice; Fr. Thomas Brennan, who died in 1972 after endearing himself to many student-athletes as a logic professor and sports chaplain; and Fr. Riehle.

When Fr. Riehle's name was added to the scholarship fund, his role in amassing money to fund the educations of students gained recognition.

"The Brennan Boland Fund is the crown jewel of the Monogram Club," said Marty Allen, in announcing at the club's annual meeting on June 3, 2004, that Fr. Riehle's name would be added.

"When Fr. Riehle became the fund's executive secretary in 1971, it had just $78,000," Allen said. Fr. Riehle boosted the total into the millions of dollars before he left his leadership role.

"As head of the Monogram Club, he [Fr. Riehle] was desirous of building up the level of participation in that part of Notre Dame," former Notre Dame President Fr. Edward "Monk" Malloy said. "He was an avid golfer, so one of the events that he was always connected with was the spring golf tournament."

That Monogram Club fundraising golf tournament became so closely identified with Fr. Riehle that the spring tradition now is called the Riehle Open in honor of the late chaplain.

At Monogram Club board meetings open to all of the members, he always would give announcements about various kinds of tournament-related achievements that merited recognition, Fr. Malloy said. The categories included low score, longest drive, etc. Attendees enjoyed him showcasing his personality at those once a year gatherings, Fr. Malloy added.

Fr. Riehle loved raising money for the club's scholarship fund to help additional students finance their way through Notre Dame.

Fr. Riehle's decision to become a clergyman "later in life," after working in the business world, gave the priest practical knowledge and administrative skills that he put to good use, Fr. Malloy said.

"I think that helped to shape his view of reality," Fr. Malloy said. The sports chaplain had gained exposure to sides of life that many clergymen may have lacked.

As a result, he possessed a first-hand understanding of the real-world challenges faced by the people who came to him for help. As a former salesman, Fr. Riehle naturally not only knew how to speak convincingly but how to allow others to share their concerns.

People used to say he had the ideal job: serving as chaplain for the football team and playing golf as the executive director of the Monogram Club, Fr. Malloy said.

"Before that, he had done a lot of difficult things on behalf of the university," Fr. Malloy said.

Watching out for Walsh

Brian "Dukie" Walsh, the all-time points leader in Notre Dame hockey history and a member of the class of 1977, remembered Fr. Riehle fondly as the team's chaplain and called him a "wonderful, genuine man."

The irony is that Walsh and his teammates also needed a firm disciplinarian at times and Fr. Riehle was the one who "kept us in line, believe me," Walsh said. Since the chaplain traveled with the team and was well acquainted with the players, he monitored them closely to ensure if they began to stray, he could intervene quickly.

"He held us all to the same standard," Walsh said.

Fr. Riehle's role went far beyond saying Masses and praying.

"In my sophomore year, I was struggling a bit academically," Walsh said. "He told me to get extra help, go to class, pay attention and do your homework."

At the start of the season, Fr. Riehle would address the standards every player on the team needed to meet.

"Boys, here is what is expected of you," Walsh recalled Fr. Riehle saying.

Academic Enforcer

Fr. Riehle also would follow up to ensure all of the players were fulfilling their academic obligations.

"He would call around and make sure we were doing well in the class-room," Walsh said.

If a problem was developing, Fr. Riehle would not hesitate to take action.

"He was tough in a caring way," Walsh said. "He'd challenge you on things. If he thought you were not living up to the standards of the team or the university, he let you know it."

Notre Dame had a higher academic standard than the NCAA to stay eligible to play varsity sports, Walsh recalled. University policy states that all continuing undergraduate students must maintain a cumulative grade-point average of at least 2.0.

For athletes who needed to compete on the playing field, Fr. Riehle told them to prepare well, play hard and stay within the rules, Walsh said.

"You can go to the edge but not go over," Walsh recalled Fr. Riehle saying.

In sports and in life, there are consequences for improper conduct.

"Hockey is a great teacher," Walsh said. "If you go off sides, the whistle blows."

Irish Fighting on the Ice

During one road game in Denver, Walsh ended up in a fight and was ejected. The game misconduct for fighting during the Friday night contest also meant Walsh would miss the following night's game against the

University of Denver. Fr. Riehle talked to Walsh afterward about the situation and the need to maintain self-control to avoid hurting his team.

"He could curse like a trucker," Walsh said. "It was never for effect. It always had a meaning."

The tough love showed by the chaplain helped to remind Walsh that the team came first. When representing Notre Dame, standards needed to be maintained.

"Fr. Riehle loved God, country and Notre Dame," Walsh said.

As Walsh recalled, Fr. Riehle "caught us all in compromising situations," whether it involved missing curfew on hockey team road trips, sneaking beers into the room at a dorm or breaking other rules.

"Fr. Riehle was pretty worldly for a priest," Walsh said. "He had a way of making sure that you did the right thing."

On the other hand, the chaplain remained available to talk and to guide. His traveling with the hockey team on road trips offered opportunities to help mold the teenagers who arrived as freshmen to become decent men.

"You could go to Fr. Jim for anything," Walsh said. "He would give it to you straight. You could talk to Fr. Riehle as if you were in confession."

Fr. Riehle's belated entrance into the seminary gave him a wealth of experiences that made his counsel especially insightful and practical, Walsh said.

"He only had your interests, the good of the team and the university in mind," Walsh said. "I don't think he ever did anything self-promotional. It was never about what he was doing. It was about what we were trying to accomplish."

Fr. Riehle to the Rescue

Once when Walsh ended up in trouble as a student at Morrissey Hall, a meeting took place with the rector of his residence hall and other people, including Fr. Riehle, about whether the student would be forced to move off campus.

The meeting took place during the 1975-76 school year and Walsh said he learned that Fr. Riehle stood up unequivocally for him. Fr. Riehle convinced the others, especially the recalcitrant rector, not to kick him out. Not only was Fr. Riehle the hockey team's chaplain, but the rector of Pangborn Hall.

When the meeting was not going well for Walsh, Fr. Riehle voiced his unflinching support by saying, "I'll take Brian tomorrow."

Based on the confident reassurance from Fr. Riehle, the rector of Morrissey Hall agreed to let Walsh stay and the student improved his behavior to justify receiving the additional chance.

At the same time, Fr. Riehle was a staunch advocate of pointing out a student's mistake as a way to learn from it. He also would tell the student firmly not to let it happen again.

When Walsh once asked Fr. Riehle what part of serving as dean of students gave him the most satisfaction, the priest replied that of all of the students who he needed to reprimand by suspending them for at least a semester, if not a full year, every one of them returned and graduated from the school, Walsh said.

"If you corrected the problem, he wanted you back at Notre Dame," Walsh said.

Housing Project Past

Without Fr. Riehle, Walsh's success at Notre Dame and beyond may not have been realized. As the first person in his family to attend college, Walsh needed a strong person to help him as he adjusted to living away from his native Massachusetts for the first time. Walsh grew up in a housing project in Cambridge, Massachusetts, as one of 11 children in his family. With such a big family in a cramped space, the children needed to eat in shifts. Walsh also remembers his father working two jobs throughout his life as the family's breadwinner and insisting that his son stay at Notre Dame to earn a degree, not sign to play professional hockey before graduation.

Walsh's accomplishments at Notre Dame included earning a B.A. in economics, serving as team captain and becoming an NCAA All-American. He also still retains Notre Dame records for the most points, 234; assists, 145; and hat tricks (three goals in a game), eight.

The priest's efforts to aid Walsh produced a Notre Dame graduate who now is a business leader in the beer industry. For six years, Walsh served as president and chief executive officer (CEO) of Long Trail Brewing Company in Bridgewater Corners, Vermont, before he sold his interest in the company in 2013. In July 2013, he became chief executive officer of Pittsburgh Brewing Co., featuring the iconic "Iron City" and "Iron City Light" brands sold in 16 states. Walsh is responsible for the company's financial turnaround efforts.

Fr. Riehle's legacy also involved helping Walsh's son, Rory, who played on the Fighting Irish hockey team as a goalie before he graduated in 2006. Rory Walsh gained some financial aid in paying for his Notre Dame studies from the Brennan-Boland-Riehle Fund. That fund is the one that Fr. Riehle was instrumental in building to become self-sustaining and expanding it to include financial assistance for the children of former Notre Dame athletes beyond the football program. The elder Walsh had contributed to the fund since his graduation, never expecting that one of his two children might attend Notre Dame, let alone compete in hockey. Brian and Rory Walsh share the distinction of becoming the first father and son to play for the Notre Dame hockey team.

Confrontation with 'Crazylegs'

An entertaining story that former Notre Dame hockey coach Charles "Lefty" Smith liked to tell involved Fr. Riehle's verbal sparring with the late University of Wisconsin Athletic Director Elroy "Crazylegs" Hirsch in between periods of a hotly contested hockey game pitting the host Badgers against Notre Dame. The snapshot in time reflects the priest's competitive spirit. Since Fr. Riehle was a former soldier and a good athlete who played a physical style of hockey, he was not at all intimidated. As a former elite football player, Hirsch also was capable of feistiness.

"One of the guys who I played with back in the dark ages was now the hockey coach at the University of Wisconsin," Smith remembered. "So, we started playing Wisconsin and eventually joined the same league. It was a very spirited rivalry to say the least. Games were always extremely hot and heavy, you might say."

Hirsch, known as "Crazylegs" because of a unique running style in which his legs seemed to move in different directions at the same time, served as Wisconsin's athletic director for 18 years. He started that job in 1969 and eliminated a $200,000 debt largely caused by sagging football attendance due to a 20-game losing streak. The former star collegiate and professional football player's presence and business acumen helped to revive the university's athletic department.

For Hirsch, his ascension to become the Wisconsin athletic director probably originated with his accomplishments on the football field. Hirsch only played one season at Wisconsin but was a standout. In 1942, he rushed for 786 yards in leading the Badgers to an 8-1-1 record. He then joined the Marines during World War II and was sent to the University of Michigan for training. At Michigan, he became the only athlete in the school's history to letter in four different sports, football, basketball, track and baseball, in one year. Hirsch was an All-American football player at both Wisconsin and Michigan.

Hostile Hosts?

Between the 1967-68 and 1997-98 seasons, the Dane County Coliseum near the Wisconsin campus served as the home rink for the university's hockey team. The venue required a visiting team to leave its bench after each period and pass through a "blue line room" where students and anybody else of legal drinking age could buy and consume beer.

"As a coach and as a chaplain, we had to walk through there to get to the locker room," Smith recalled.

One time while navigating that journey through the beer-drinking fans, Smith said he reached the locker room but the chaplain did not. Soon thereafter, a knock was heard at the door. Someone told Smith he needed to come out to retrieve his team chaplain. Hirsch attended Wisconsin's hockey game against Notre Dame that evening and participated in a spontaneous conversation with the chaplain of the Fighting Irish team that turned heated. The priest and the rival team's athletic director were airing their differences of opinion in full public view.

The verbal exchange occurred in an open concourse in the presence of hostile Wisconsin Badger fans. Fr. Riehle was undeterred, even though the Badger backers in the vicinity were becoming boisterous while indulging in the beverages produced by the state's breweries. Smith found and escorted the chaplain into the locker room and away from the raucous atmosphere where Hirsch learned that Fr. Riehle was no wimp.

"Everybody was afraid that he [the chaplain] was going to punch him," Smith recalled with a chuckle. "So, we had to settle him down and get him out of there and get him into the locker room where he could be safe."

If the team's chaplain had punched the athletic director at the University of Wisconsin, "it would not have gone over too well," said Smith, who remembered the combustible situation ending harmlessly. On the other hand, it could have carried unmistakable impact in reinforcing Notre Dame's nickname, the "Fighting Irish." It also is not beyond the realm of possibility that Hirsch may have engaged in verbal repartee with the Notre Dame chaplain deliberately to promote a growing hockey rivalry between the two schools to help spur ticket sales to future games.

Senior Chivalry

After spending three years at Breen-Phillips Hall, Bob Thomas, the kicker for Notre Dame's football team between 1971 and 1973, and the other men who had lived in that dormitory, needed to move elsewhere for a history-making reason. The place that they considered home during the previous school year was converted into a residence hall for women during fall 1973, the year after Notre Dame began admitting female undergraduates. In previous years, a senior would have received first choice of the dorm rooms at the residence hall where he lived.

The men who had lived at Breen-Phillips Hall learned that they would move to Lyons Hall when they returned to school in the fall. The incoming students received word that they would enter into a lottery to determine their room assignments, without regard to seniority.

As a result, seniors from Breen-Phillips participated in the lottery with the residents of Lyons Hall and the unlucky ones ended up in flawed rooms that many other students had passed up in favor of more inviting accommodations. According to the University of Notre Dame's website, the architecture of Lyons Hall creates "many unique room configurations."

Lottery Losers

Thomas and his roommate, Finn McDavid, lost the lottery. They found themselves stuck with a dingy, cramped, overheated and windowless basement dorm room in Lyons Hall. As someone who won his spot on the team as a walk-on player, Thomas was not a pampered athlete. However, no senior could have expected to find himself at the bottom of the dorm-room pecking order.

"We were one of the last ones to get to pick a room," Thomas said. "And what was left, from my recollection, were rooms basically in the basement with heating pipes going through them and everything else. I remember the room being about 95 degrees."

Thomas, who later played 12 seasons in the National Football League before becoming an Illinois Supreme Court justice, quickly sized up the situation and knew he faced an unpleasant and uncomfortable school year, without corrective action taking place quickly. With the football season about to begin and Thomas desperate for help, he placed a phone call to Fr. Riehle to share his unhappiness about the dismal living conditions.

"In telling him, I think he thought it might impact adversely on my psyche as far as going on and kicking field goals for the Irish," Thomas said.

Reaching out to Fr. Riehle

Within 24 hours, Fr. Riehle arranged for Thomas and his roommate to move to a bigger room on an upper floor in Grace Hall, an 11-story tower that was one of the most modern dormitories on campus. Not only did that room have windows, but a splendid view of the outdoors. For a student who lived in university housing, the move was comparable to going from the poorhouse to the penthouse.

"We went from having what I think was one of the worst rooms on campus to one of the best," Thomas said. "I don't know how he [Fr. Riehle] pulled it off, but he pulled it off."

The dorm room at Grace Hall, opened just four years earlier in 1969, was a "double" that was built and equipped for two students, rather than the living unit they left behind in Lyons Hall that Thomas said resembled a "little room in a submarine." In addition, the two-man room at Grace Hall had modern desks and its own heating and air conditioning unit.

"It was quite a dramatic difference between having a year living at Grace versus where they had planned to put us at Lyons," Thomas said.

While other students may have gone to the director of the residence hall for help, Thomas remembered why he chose Fr. Riehle to intervene.

Reverend to the Rescue

"He was the chaplain of the team and obviously cared about the players on the team," Thomas said. "We were his group of guys. He prayed with us before games and after games. We would see in him the locker room every week and on the sidelines at practice. So, I thought that I would just tell him of the problem."

Characteristically, Fr. Riehle did not say much but he promised to help and took quick action.

"It was basically, 'Don't worry about it; I'll handle it,'" Thomas recalled Fr. Riehle telling him. "And he certainly did."

Few would have guessed at the time that Fr. Riehle was interceding for the player on the team who would score the winning points in the national championship football game just months later. Thomas booted a 19-yard field goal in the waning minutes of the Sugar Bowl to lift Notre Dame to a 24-23 win against the University of Alabama Crimson Tide.

"It had rained all that day," Thomas said in describing the sloppy field conditions.

Tide Turned Back

The precipitation bedeviled the kickers and holders on both teams at the Sugar Bowl. However, Thomas delivered in the clutch to propel Notre Dame to finish its season 11-0 with its upset victory against Alabama in the bowl game at Tulane Stadium in New Orleans on December 31, 1973.

The 1973 Fighting Irish team became the university's ninth football squad to win a national championship and the second of Parseghian's nine-year tenure as the head coach. Parseghian's best call during the game may have come with a little more than two minutes left on third down and eight yards to go for a first down, with Notre Dame pinned deep in its in own territory near the two-year-line. Robin Weber, a backup tight end who primarily served as a blocker, broke free from the Alabama defense for a 37-yard gain when he caught a pass thrown from the back of the end zone by Tom Clements, Notre Dame's quarterback.

Fr. Riehle's best call that season might have been the one he placed to help Thomas change his dorm room.

Last-Chance Chaplain

Without Fr. Riehle's help, former defensive lineman Tom "Big T" Ross said he would not have received his diploma from Notre Dame.

"When I graduated, I received my diploma envelope from Fr. Hesburgh," Ross said. "When I opened it, it was blank. There was a note saying I owed $147 for hall damage and unpaid parking tickets. About five years or so later, I stopped by Fr. Riehle's office."

Fr. Riehle listened to Ross explain what happened and agreed to accept a reduced amount to resolve the bill.

"We negotiated a settlement for half of the amount, so I could get my diploma and transcripts," Ross said. "We had a good laugh about it and

I brought up that story during my [Monogram Club] acceptance speech in 1999."

Perturbed Parents

Fr. Riehle's intervention brought happiness to far more people than just Ross. His graduation on August 9, 1974, was the same day that Richard Nixon resigned as president. With Ross focused on his wedding the next day at the Basilica of the Sacred Heart, he was not particularly distressed that he did not receive his diploma. However, other members of his family reacted differently.

"My parents were disappointed," Ross said.

Fr. Riehle characteristically resolved the problem and lightened the mood with his sense of humor in the process. It also turned into yet another occasion when Fr. Riehle helped a football coach.

"My father, William 'Bill' Ross, was Joe Namath's football coach," said Ross, whose dad coached the future Super Bowl winner when he was a sophomore at Beaver Falls High School in Pennsylvania. Namath, then 5'7" and 135 lbs., contemplated quitting football that season but Coach Ross convinced him to keep trying.

The story of that pivotal time in Namath's life was shared by the quarterback in an August 2010 *ESPN The Magazine* article. Namath told his coach that he planned to give up football and focus on basketball. Coach Ross told the then-undersized Namath that he still could become a special player, reminded him that he was just a sophomore and persuaded him to reconsider.

"My dad was the nicest guy I've ever known," Ross said. "Ironically, I am older now than he was when he died June 11, 1976, at age 55. The good do die young. Duke and I will live forever!"

Exclusive Deal

Fr. Riehle stood out for his contributions to the development of young men and women, particularly student-athletes, said Darrell "Flash" Gordon, a former outside linebacker at Notre Dame and now the CEO of Wernle

Youth and Family Treatment Center in Richmond, Indiana. However, the priest's leadership extended well beyond sports.

"We produced both on and off the field at Notre Dame and one of the reasons was the influence of Fr. Riehle," Gordon said.

On many occasions when Fr. Riehle happened to be at practice or some other place, Gordon said he would ask the chaplain for a prayer. As that interaction may suggest, Gordon said that they had a strong connection.

"He was committed to me and I felt like it was personally to me," Gordon said. "He made you feel like it was you he was committed to in helping to achieve success."

Fr. Riehle also served as a confidant in place of a mother or a father for students on campus.

People do business with you if they think you are offering them the best "deal" exclusively and that is the kind of impression that Fr. Riehle could give, Gordon said. With Fr. Riehle, the "deal" involved spiritual intervention through prayers and blessings.

Target for Teasing

"We used to always tease him," Gordon said. "If there is only one job in the world that any man would want, it would be to become the chaplain for the football team at Notre Dame."

Imagine spending a Saturday in the fall as Fr. Riehle did. He enjoyed a sideline view of Notre Dame's football game from the 50-yard line, while standing next to the team's head coach. The chaplain offered a pre-game Mass and prayed "grace" before college football's "best pre-game meal," which typically consisted of steak and shrimp, Gordon said.

Fr. Riehle also traveled with the team to every game.

"There was no better job at Notre Dame than being the head chaplain in athletics," Gordon said. "Fr. Riehle had a front seat of everything in life."

As the football chaplain, it also was Fr. Riehle's duty to deliver a pre-game prayer, just as he personally did in the movie *Rudy,* to prepare the team to take the field.

For most college teams, the head coach is the key motivator. At Notre Dame, Fr. Riehle's pre-game Mass and prayer carried great importance, despite their brevity.

Before the game, "you heard his prayer," Gordon said. "Pray for us," Gordon recalled Fr. Riehle saying. In his prayer, Fr. Riehle voiced an ardent appeal for the players to use their athletic talents for God's purposes.

"It was like he wanted to get onto the field and play," Gordon said.

Miami Hurricanes

The unique pre-game role that Fr. Riehle played with the Notre Dame football team may have been best exemplified by his motivational words to the players just before the 1988 kick off in South Bend, Indiana, against the University of Miami Hurricanes. Notre Dame's path to a national championship that season required beating the University of Miami, the defending national champion. Both teams entered the game undefeated but the University of Miami had won four straight games against Notre Dame, including a 24-0 shutout of the Fighting Irish during the previous season.

A number of the University of Miami players seemed to take pride in trying to intimidate their opponents with trash talking, physical play and on-field behavior that might be considered outright taunting. In fact, the University of Miami's 46-3 win against the University of Texas in the 1991 Cotton Bowl featured 16 penalties for the Hurricanes, including nine for unsportsmanlike conduct. Just months later, the NCAA instituted a 15-yard penalty for any player who engaged in prolonged celebrations or taunting.

In contrast, Notre Dame teams are coached to conduct themselves with dignity and to display good sportsmanship, Gordon said.

If anyone crosses the goal line to score a touchdown, Coach Holtz would say to "act like you've been there before," Gordon said.

"While warming up, I can remember seeing Fr. Riehle," Gordon said.

The Miami players headed toward the tunnel under the stadium to return to the visitors' locker room but they chose to cut directly through a line of Notre Dame players "disrespectfully" rather than go around them as other teams typically would have done, Gordon recalled. Physical contact ensued and escalated quickly. The confrontation between the players on both teams came to a boil within seconds.

Pre-Game Punches

"That was as much as we could take," Gordon said. "Then there was a big brawl."

When the melee ended, the players returned "bloodied and bruised" to their respective locker rooms before the game, Gordon said.

Notre Dame's players felt that they had to defend themselves.

"They wanted to totally take our manhood and disrespect us," Gordon said.

Wary about whether Fr. Riehle would criticize the players for engaging in a pre-game scrap, despite the provocation of bullying opponents, Gordon said that the chaplain instead made sure that the Fighting Irish returned to the field focused and ready to play.

"I don't believe the way they conduct themselves," Gordon recalled Fr. Riehle saying in the locker room about the Miami team after the altercation. "They deserve to be put in their place. You had to do what you had to do."

Those words helped to rally and to prepare the team.

"Ultimately, you've got to fight for what is right," Gordon said. "It was like God saying, 'Son, you just did what you had to do.'"

Gordon also remembered Fr. Riehle's final words before the team returned to the field.

"Now, gentlemen, go out there and start this game," Gordon recalled Fr. Riehle saying.

As usual, Fr. Riehle's words inspired the team.

Notre Dame's professorial-looking Head Coach Lou Holtz sounded as fired up as his players when he followed Fr. Riehle's words prior to leaving the locker room for the opening kick-off by telling everyone present to "save" the Hurricanes' Head Coach Jimmy Johnson for him, Gordon recalled.

Avenging Athletes

Johnson, a highly successful football coach at the University of Miami, sparked controversy during his team's 1985 victory against the Fighting Irish when the Hurricanes tacked on points in the waning minutes to pad the margin of victory against Notre Dame to 55-7. That 1985 game was the last one at the university for then-Coach Gerry Faust. Gordon was among many Notre Dame players on the 1988 team who endured the drubbing in 1985.

Inspired by Fr. Riehle, the Notre Dame players headed onto the field in 1988 to compete in a hotly contested and physical football game. Notre Dame won 31-30 by forcing the high-powered University of Miami team into seven turnovers and stopping a two-point conversion attempt at the end of the game when defensive back Pat Terrell knocked down a pass in the end zone to preserve the victory.

Whatever one's view about the two schools, news media accounts after the game described the clash as the Catholics against the "Convicts." Gordon and a number of his teammates avenged previous defeats against Miami with the huge 1988 win.

Competitive Chaplain

Fr. Riehle's uplifting words fit with his duties as the team chaplain.

"He was spiritual, fair and in tune with making sure that you didn't get pushed around on the field," Gordon said.

Fr. Riehle understood that the players needed to be competitive but he also put "things in perspective" for the 18-, 19- and 20-year-old student-athletes at Notre Dame, Gordon said.

"I believe the support is never better than what you get from Christ and a gentleman who speaks on His behalf," Gordon said.

The questionable behavior of a number of Miami players at that 1988 game became a rallying moment for the Notre Dame team and a turning point at the university that led to a "decade of great football," Gordon said.

Fr. Riehle contributed to and endorsed the process of returning the football program to a place among the nation's elite teams, Gordon said.

Rockne-like Response

Fr. Riehle's unforgettable words deepened the resolve of the Notre Dame players to excel. The University of Miami Hurricanes football team entered its 1988 game against Notre Dame aware that the Fighting Irish possessed a potent pass rush.

The key challenge for the Miami offense that day would be "pass protection," recalled Steve Walsh, the starting quarterback of the Hurricanes.

Unknown to Walsh and his Miami teammates was that their team's pre-game behavior gave Fr. Riehle an unexpected opportunity to fire up the Notre Dame players. Since the University of Miami in recent years had not just beaten Notre Dame but padded the margin of victory with late-game scores, Fr. Riehle understood that the team he led spiritually was at a crossroads as it attempted to reemerge as a national football power. It may have been one of the most important occasions that Fr. Riehle addressed the players during the decades he served as a Notre Dame sports chaplain.

Walsh acknowledged the significance that a chaplain can play in influencing the players on a football team. Walsh, a Catholic who quarterbacked the Miami team that gained the nickname "Convicts" for its unruly actions, said he understood how a team chaplain could help players to set aside distractions just before kick-off.

The fight before the Notre Dame game was another in a series of confrontations that the University of Miami players had with opposing teams that strayed outside of good sportsmanship. Walsh said his Miami teammates tried to motivate themselves with their behavior. They also recognized the need to protect their starting quarterback during the brawl that they initiated with Notre Dame's players.

"I had, like, four freshmen [teammates] surrounding me," Walsh said. "I didn't throw a single punch. I was kind of laughing the whole time."

Walsh remembered the circumstances leading up to the altercation and acknowledged that some of his University of Miami teammates triggered the fracas. His Miami team had just finished its pre-game warm-ups.

Suddenly, a Miami player asked a provocative question about whether they should go through or around a line of Notre Dame players who were conducting pre-game drills on the football field.

"What do you want to do?" Walsh said one of his teammates inquired aloud. "Somebody said, 'Go through 'em.' That's what precipitated the fight. We went through their drill or their stretch line or something like that."

Spontaneous Eruption

The fight was not pre-mediated, Walsh said. It occurred spontaneously when the Miami players headed toward the Notre Dame Stadium's tunnel to return to the locker room, he explained.

"Chalk it up to bad design of the stadium," said Walsh, deflecting the blame for the fight from his teammates.

"I know the guys who were the instigators," Walsh said. "I just kind of let them do their thing. They knew it was going to create a reaction. So, it was a calculated move. Obviously, it didn't work out. We didn't win. It's not something that we did contemplate."

For many years, the University of Miami football teams became known for behavior that crossed the line into outright taunting of their opponents.

"When you think back to my time there, '85-'88, in all the big games, there was some jawing and there was some pushing and shoving after the whistle, and even before games," Walsh said.

The Miami players realized that the 1988 contest against Notre Dame was a "big game," Walsh said.

"We knew what was at stake," Walsh recalled.

So did Fr. Riehle, who found a way to spark Notre Dame after the pre-game fight. Walsh expressed an appreciation for a football chaplain's value. He spoke highly of the University of Miami's one-time Catholic Chaplain, Fr. Leo Armbrust, who served in that role between 1983 and 1996.

"We had probably 20-25 Catholics on our team," Walsh said. "It could have been as many [Catholics] as Notre Dame. I don't know. We said Catholic Mass before every one of our games."

Fr. Armbrust also was a "very dynamic leader," who gave plenty of "pep talks, too," Walsh said.

"That's why the whole Catholics vs. Convicts thing was kind of comical to me," Walsh said.

One difference is that all of the Notre Dame football players and coaches attend a pre-game Catholic Mass, not just the Catholics. As a result, the entire Notre Dame team heard Fr. Riehle explain how that particular game would let them exhibit their God-given talents. Regardless of the Scripture readings of a given day, Fr. Riehle always found a way to use them to prepare the players for their game.

Notre Dame Reminders

Walsh has become accustomed to discussing the 1988 loss to Notre Dame and the role of team chaplains.

"We have pre-game Mass at our high school," said Walsh, who now coaches at Cardinal Newman High School in West Palm Beach, Florida.

Ironically, the president of the high school is Fr. David Carr, a Catholic priest and a 1973 graduate of the University of Notre Dame. In Fr. Carr's office at the high school is an image of Notre Dame's Leprechaun, Walsh said.

"I have to put up with that every day when I go to visit with him," Walsh said.

It seems Walsh cannot avoid regular reminders of Notre Dame that inevitably conjure up memories of the one game that he and his Miami teammates lost in 1988 that propelled Notre Dame to the national title that year. It also marked the fourth time Fr. Riehle served as chaplain of a national championship football team.

"They deserved the national championship," Walsh said. "Obviously, we would have loved to play them again. They were certainly a good football team... a great football team."

Transforming Lives

Fr. Riehle also served as a role model in the way he devoted himself to help young people. Gordon said that the lessons he learned at Notre Dame from Fr. Riehle and others prepared him to become a leader of a child development center, where he seeks to assist the children in the program to become "more powerful people."

"If something is going to change, you need to be involved in changing it," Gordon said. "The reason I am probably where I am today is not simply because of my family, but because of Notre Dame, spiritually, academically and athletically."

Gordon leads the Wernle Youth and Family Treatment Center in Richmond, Indiana, where hundreds of boys are aided each year with mental health issues, as well as substance abuse struggles.

"We provide counseling for not only the boys, but their families, as well," Gordon said. "Sometimes, for the first time in their lives, they learn to trust adults and are given the hope and ability to achieve the goals in their lives that they desire. Our mission is to rebuild relationships and restore hope. Shouldn't that be what we all strive to do? I can say with confidence that Fr. Riehle's mission is parallel to ours in restoring hope to many young athletes who contemplate their true purpose in life."

Gordon grew up in an urban environment that had a dearth of mentors for neighborhood children. His childhood was spent away from the affluent side of his hometown of Hillside, New Jersey. His household included a single-parent mother, four brothers and two sisters.

To develop toughness as a boy, Gordon did not need to leave the front door of his house. The second-oldest brother in the family was a Golden Gloves welter-weight boxer. Gordon's youngest brother became the captain of the Brown University football team. Gordon, the second-youngest boy in the family, had good athletes in his own household who helped him to develop into a starting linebacker on Notre Dame's 1988 national title team.

But Gordon's mother ensured that her children gained exposure to values in life that transcended athletics.

"My mom was extremely spiritual," Gordon said. She would "drag me along" to church activities all the time, he added.

"That set the foundation for when I got to Notre Dame to understand the value of spirituality," Gordon said. "That five-year experience set my life up for the future successes that I've had."

Paying Back

Rather than pursue the most lucrative career possible, Gordon is working at a faith-based, Lutheran agency that has a mission of helping children to transform their lives.

Indeed, Gordon once worked on Wall Street, earned a law degree, practiced at a large law firm and took graduate-level courses in strategic planning at Harvard University. Despite other career options, the father of two children chose to head a child development center.

"I'm giving back because it is what is expected of us at Notre Dame," Gordon said. "I have had the opportunity to do pretty much anything that I wanted to do. Spiritually, sometimes we have callings and it is incumbent upon us to respond."

In that sense, Gordon said he is helping young people just as Fr. Riehle did. With Fr. Riehle as the athletics chaplain and Fr. George Rozum as the rector of his Alumni Hall dormitory at Notre Dame, Gordon said he had the benefit of good spiritual leaders.

Fr. Riehle's queries to students about how their classes were going showed that he valued education, Gordon said.

"We all had water-fountain conversations heading on and off the field," Gordon said. "I always would talk to Fr. Riehle. He would sit in his golf cart on the practice field, in case anybody needed anything spiritually."

Motivational Mentor

"I'm always coaching young men to do great things and perform at their highest levels, even with challenges," Gordon said. "I try to provide hope for young men who typically would not have it."

The child development center helps boys, for example, who need to overcome conditions such as Asperger syndrome, which is manifested through poor concentration, a tendency to withdraw socially, difficulty learning in group settings, delayed development of motor skills and extreme disorganization. However, those challenges can be ameliorated with treatment.

Regardless of a child's ability, proper guidance can be useful in improving performance. As a volunteer football coach, Gordon said that he attempts to encourage the kids to play "at the highest level" that they can for all four quarters of a game, just as Fr. Riehle did in his role as an athletic chaplain.

If a coach can accomplish that goal, the kids will stay motivated to give their best for "the rest of the season," said Gordon, who expressed hope that athletic field accomplishments could carry over to encourage children to "fulfill their potential" in other ways.

Oliver's Final Farewell

Fr. Riehle's example of giving blessings was put into practice by Gerry Faust when the former Notre Dame football coach arrived minutes after Fighting Irish kicking hero Harry Oliver died of cancer at the age of 47 on August 8, 2007. Faust had rushed to his former player's bedside after learning that Oliver was close to death. Faust gave his own blessing by patting Oliver's left leg. It was Oliver's kicking leg. The pat resembled the way that Fr. Riehle used to bless a player.

The now-retired coach, who left Notre Dame with a winning but unspectacular 30-26-1 record after five seasons to become the head coach at Akron University, said Oliver stands out as one of the finest people who ever played for him.

"He was extremely close to the Lord," Faust said about Oliver. "If he's not with God, no one is."

Those that viewed Oliver as an unforgettable hero who relied on his faith for strength went well beyond his former coach. Oliver was a high school soccer player when Faust discovered him. As the head coach at Cincinnati's Moeller High School, Faust urged Oliver to kick for the Catholic school's championship football team. When Oliver became a high school senior, Faust persuaded then-Notre Dame Head Coach Dan Devine to offer Oliver a full scholarship as a placekicker.

Faust shared one of his favorite stories with the kicker's family, shortly after Oliver died. With friends and family still surrounding the bed, Faust described taking his Moeller High School football team to the Pro Football Hall of Fame in Canton, Ohio. The visit took place on the same Saturday as the 1980 Notre Dame-Michigan football game when Fr. Riehle was the team chaplain. Moeller players and coaches gathered near a television set to watch the end of the game with the Fighting Irish trailing, 27-26. The outcome depended on whether Moeller graduate Oliver could kick the longest field goal of his life in the game's waning seconds. Oliver shocked Michigan and amazed Notre Dame fans by booting a seemingly miraculous 51-yard field goal to win the game. The Moeller players celebrated with the enthusiasm of teenagers.

A Hall of Fame representative observed the Moeller players revel after watching one of their own graduates lead Notre Dame to victory in a game that appeared to be lost. Moments later, the Hall of Fame official told Faust that his players must be among Notre Dame's most devoted fans.

"Not only do they love Notre Dame," Faust said he replied, "but they are Harry Oliver fans!"

Lasting Legend

Oliver's family members laughed and smiled upon hearing the story at their loved one's bedside just minutes after he had taken his last breath. Oliver's game-winning field goal to beat Michigan spurred Devine to call Faust the day after the game to thank the high school coach for recommending the kicker three years earlier. Oliver was beaten out for the starting job during his first two years at Notre Dame but he kept working at his craft and rewarded Devine by delivering the clutch field goal against Michigan on the last play of the unforgettable 1980 game.

Ironically, only an injury to another Notre Dame kicker, Steve Cichy, put Oliver onto the field to try the game-clinching kick. The moment when Oliver headed onto the gridiron for the final play is etched in the memory of his former Notre Dame roommate Mike Wojciak, who became an optometrist in the Chicago area. The field goal needed to be kicked from such a great distance that none of Oliver's friends in the stands anticipated that he would be called upon. Oliver's specialty was kicking shorter field goals, not booming long ones.

"It was so far, I don't think anybody even expected them to send Harry out to try the kick," Wojciak said.

Oliver, a mechanical engineering student, became an unlikely hero. He left the field in glory, despite his earlier miss of an extra point that put Notre Dame behind by one point when he ran onto the field for the final play.

"Father Riehle must have sent a few 'Hail Mary's' Harry's way before the kick," Wojciak said.

Day of Destiny

Fr. Riehle never prayed for victory or the outcome of a particular play. But in the case of Oliver needing to kick the ball so far, the chaplain may have prayed for the kicker to do his best.

Shortly before the end of the Notre Dame-Michigan game in which Oliver kicked his game-winning field goal, Fr. Riehle and the athletic trainer John Whitmer headed toward the stadium's tunnel leading to the locker room at the north end zone to avoid a crowd of people who would be on the field after the contest. Whitmer remembered Fr. Riehle walking several steps in front of him but they both stopped when they reached the area behind the back of the end zone to watch the game's final plays as Notre Dame advanced the ball to Michigan's 34-yard-line.

"Then, they decided to kick that field goal," Whitmer said about Notre Dame's coaches.

The wind had been gusting up to 20 mph virtually the entire game. Unless the wind stopped, Oliver would need to kick directly into a stiff breeze.

"The wind was coming out of the southwest, I believe," Whitmer said. "And, the wind just became still."

As Whitmer watched Oliver head onto the field to attempt the long field goal, he recalled telling Fr. Riehle, "Harry doesn't have that kind of range."

Upon hearing those words from Whitmer, the team trainer said Fr. Riehle looked at him, removed the cigar from his mouth, held it in his left hand, bowed his head and prayed silently for 20-25 seconds before making the sign of the cross with his right hand just prior to the field goal attempt.

When the kick cleared the cross bar of the goal posts on the south end of the field, Fr. Riehle flashed a big grin, Whitmer said. Fr. Riehle then put his cigar back into his mouth and headed happily through the tunnel to the locker room to bless each player as the team returned from the spontaneous victory celebration on the field.

"It was quite the moment," Whitmer said.

The occasion was similar to the time students chanted in unison during a home football game, "Ara, stop the rain," Whitmer said. Amazingly, the rain stopped, at least for a while.

Divine Intervention?

When Oliver stepped onto the gridiron to attempt the field goal, it was as if all the students in the stands were "holding their breath under water for the whole time," Wojciak said. The 51-yard field goal attempt was far longer than Oliver's previous best of 38 yards in a junior varsity game.

"I like to think everybody was praying for him," Wojciak said. "Everybody in the stands and all the Notre Dame fans were just praying: 'Please make this.' When the ball went through, it was mayhem."

The winning kick provided lasting inspiration to many people who witnessed the surreal scene, Wojciak said. The memorable play began with deep doubt about success, included group prayer for a miracle finish and ended with shared jubilation for the Notre Dame faithful.

"Harry's kick was a score for the underdog," Wojciak said. "I think it showed how faith and determination can pay off and last a lifetime."

Oliver only had made one varsity field goal in his entire Notre Dame career up to that point, said Wojciak, who attended the game and nearly three decades later distinctly remembered the moment when the ball cleared the goal posts' crossbar by about three inches.

For Christians who believe in the Holy Trinity, signifying the Father, the Son and the Holy Spirit, the three-inch margin of success for a seemingly heaven-sent result conjures up visions of divine intervention. The moment also marked another time when Fr. Riehle served as the team's spiritual leader at a game that seemed lost but suddenly and inexplicably ended in a dramatic Notre Dame win.

One of the 60,000-plus fans at the game was then-Notre Dame electrical engineering student Robert Whearty, who confirmed the strong wind that had blown throughout the afternoon stopping suddenly as the Fighting Irish lined up to try the game-winning field goal. Whearty said he and many other Notre Dame students shared the opinion that divine intervention determined the game's outcome. In his view, a headline in a Michigan newspaper the day after the game accurately reflected the final score: Michigan 27, Notre Dame 26, God 3.

Also in the stands watching the unforgettable conclusion to the classic game was Rep. Fred Upton, R-Michigan, who became chairman of the House Energy and Commerce Committee. The Michigan graduate's home town is St. Joseph, Michigan, a short car ride from Notre Dame's campus. He vividly remembered Oliver's game-winning kick.

"As a die-hard Maize and Blue guy who lives only a few miles from South Bend, I was at this memorable game and, yes, remember the brisk wind dying right at the moment the ball was kicked," Rep. Upton said. "My heart sank as the ball trickled through the goal posts, handing Notre Dame the victory. No question, there was more than Irish luck at play."

When kicking the game winner, the giant mosaic called "Touchdown Jesus" was behind Oliver, while the open end of the stadium faced him. Without the wind stopping, Oliver told the media he could not have kicked the ball far enough. Oliver added that he was convinced "Touchdown Jesus" helped him by nudging the ball over the cross bar.

Ball Nearly Blocked

Michigan defensive back Brian Carpenter barely missed blocking the line-drive kick with his outstretched arms and hands after racing around from the edge of the Wolverines' line and diving at the spot where he thought the ball would travel on its way toward the goal posts.

"I remember thinking that I was going to block the kick," Carpenter said. "I laid out for the ball and I thought I was going to get it. I landed on the ground and I looked up to see the ball flying through the goal posts."

The wind was blowing so strongly before the final play that Carpenter said he knew he needed to move quickly to block the kick, since the breeze would aid the ball in reaching the holder faster than normal.

"The wind died just before the snap," Carpenter recalled.

Jim Brandstatter also said he recalled noticing the wind stop while broadcasting the game as the color commentator for the University of Michigan radio network.

Lloyd Carr, who was Michigan's defensive backfield coach in his first season with the Wolverines that year, remembered watching the final play unfold before his eyes. It was his first Michigan-Notre Dame game.

As Notre Dame prepared to try a potential game-winning field goal, Carr said he remembered looking at the south end zone of Notre Dame Stadium. The flag was blowing briskly. Just before the ball was snapped for the field goal attempt, Carr recalled glancing back at the south end zone.

"That flag was limp," Carr said. "And, of course, he was kicking from the right hash mark, which made it an even more difficult kick."

When watching the football travel through the air to decide the outcome of a game, a few seconds seems like a "lifetime," Carr said. He lost sight of the ball as it headed toward the goal posts. The way he knew that the ball had cleared the cross bar successfully was when the fans in the south end zone "erupted" in unbridled excitement, he recalled. The improbable finish caused a crushing game-ending defeat for Michigan and produced what many attendees that day claim was the Lord's answer to a collective prayer from tens of thousands of Notre Dame fans who witnessed an unassuming daily churchgoer become the unlikely hero.

The irony of the wind playing a role in the outcome of the game holds significance for Christians who associate powerful winds with the Holy Spirit. According to Scripture, the Holy Spirit stayed behind when Christ ascended to heaven. If strong winds are associated with the existence of the Holy Spirit, could the abrupt ceasing of winds indicate the Holy Spirit took a role in the final play?

Heavenly Hard Drive

"It's like a picture ingrained in your memory or embedded in your hard drive," Wojciak said. "You just can't get rid of it. It changed so many people."

The winning kick turned Oliver into a Notre Dame football hero but the acclaim never changed him, Wojciak said.

"I don't ever think he realized how long what he did would last," Wojciak said.

In fact, Oliver just seemed to be happy to have contributed to a Notre Dame win, without any attention-grabbing grandstanding.

"I don't think it affected him as much as it affected other people," Wojciak said. "That was a good thing about him. He was a one-of-a-kind guy."

Prayer Power

Oliver's heroics nearly never had a chance to occur. He became dejected the previous year when his performance academically and athletically did not meet his expectations. Oliver grew so "disenchanted" that he responded by deepening his prayer life, recalled Wojciak, the kicker's roommate at Grace Hall during their freshman and sophomore years.

"He joined Opus Dei and got involved in going to Mass every day," Wojciak said.

Those efforts to find the kind of spiritual strength that Fr. Riehle encouraged led Oliver through a difficult time. Oliver returned to school for his junior year with deepened determination and seemed more focused than in the past, Wojciak said.

Unlike other football players who often were significantly bigger or clearly endowed with special strength or talent, Oliver had an unimposing physique, Wojciak said. When football players walked around campus, their confident strides and demeanor seemed to convey the impression, "Where's the water, we'll walk on it," Wojciak said.

Despite not resembling a beefy major college football player, Oliver may have had the ideal temperament to be called upon to perform in the clutch.

"Nothing fazed him," Wojciak said. Oliver's casual acceptance of his moment of glory is similar to the gentle nature and the good intentions displayed in the movie "Forrest Gump" by the main character with the same name. The fictional Forrest Gump was portrayed in an Oscar-winning performance by actor Tom Hanks.

"If you've ever seen that movie about how somebody so humble could touch so many lives and not realize the impact that he had on them, that was Harry," Wojciak said.

The same sentiment applies to Fr. Riehle, who was able to encourage and help Oliver and others spiritually when they needed it the most.

Humble Hero

The comparison between humble heroes Harry Oliver and Forrest Gump is relevant for the play in the Michigan game when the kicker turned defeat into victory. However, Oliver had a sharp mind to go along with his moment of glory. He earned his Notre Dame degree and became a professional engineer.

"Harry was very smart," Wojciak said. "The world is a better place because he was here. When I look back, other than him shutting off the lights at 9 p.m. or getting up at the crack of dawn to go to Mass when I'd come in hung over, I have nothing bad to say about him."

The other football players hung out together but Oliver blended in comfortably with virtually all of the other students who he met, Wojciak said. For that reason, it was easy for students who did not play football to relate to Oliver. He seemed to be just another student trying to survive the rigorous academic requirements of Notre Dame to earn a degree.

"From throwing water balloons out the 11th floor study hall window at us or dropping water balloons out the window on him, he was just one of the guys," Wojciak said with a laugh.

Faust's admiration for Oliver, a devout Catholic who tried to attend Mass each day amid Fr. Riehle's spiritual influence, did not hinge on whether his kicker succeeded in each field goal attempt. The year after Oliver beat Michigan, Faust became Notre Dame's head coach in an unconventional ascension. It is extremely rare for a high school coach to become head coach at a major university without any intermediate stops in between. Faust's hiring may have been the greatest challenge ever faced by a high school coach in attempting to make such a daunting transition. He confronted immediate pressure to succeed at possibly the most storied college football program in the country.

Early Intervention

Faust credited Fr. Riehle for aiding in his adjustment. Fr. Riehle also counseled the coach when the disappointment of losing more games than expected led to mounting pressures. In the first months of Faust's tenure at Notre Dame, Fr. Theodore Hesburgh, the university's president, left a message asking the coach to join him for lunch on a particular date. Faust already had scheduled an out-of-town recruiting visit that day, so he relayed word that he would be unavailable to meet Fr. Hesburgh and suggested an alternative date. It turned out to be the first time in 35 years at the helm of the university that Fr. Hesburgh had anyone turn down a lunch invitation with him. Faust needed a mentor and Fr. Riehle filled the void.

Within days, Fr. Riehle appeared at the coach's door. It was a Friday afternoon and high school football recruits were arriving. Fr. Riehle used a bit of humor in recalling Fr. Hesburgh's version of the story. During the previous Sunday evening, Fr. Hesburgh shared a meal with his fellow priests and drew laughter from everyone there by explaining how the new football coach informed the university president that his lunch invitation could not be accepted due to a previously scheduled recruiting trip.

Upon learning from Fr. Riehle that the coach had become the first person in 35 years to decline a lunch invitation from the university's president, Faust said he rescheduled his recruiting trip and called Fr. Hesburgh's office to accept the offer. During that lunch, Fr. Hesburgh shared with the coach a brief synopsis of every Notre Dame football coach in modern times. Fr. Hesburgh described the key strengths and weaknesses of each of them, Faust said. It turned out to be an extremely informative, three-hour meeting that the coach said he remembered decades later. Faust left the lunch appreciating how important it was for Fr. Riehle to have persuaded him by using levity to convince the coach to accept the invitation at the appointed time.

"He [Fr. Jim] helped me all five years I was there," Faust said. "He was a close confidant and a great priest."

Mike Brey, Notre Dame's head men's basketball coach, said Fr. Riehle reached out to him upon his arrival at Notre Dame in 2000.

"I met Father Riehle as a young head coach on the college level," Brey said. "He mentored me in the ways of Notre Dame, making sure I knew how special this place is and to cherish it."

Brey also said Fr. Riehle urged him to "be yourself," which is the same advice that the coach received from his mentor Morgan Wootten, a legendary basketball coach at DeMatha High School in Hyattsville, Maryland. Brey played for Wootten and later became his assistant coach before going to Duke University as an assistant coach for Mike Krzyzewski.

Chapter 6

EXERT EFFORT TO OVERCOME OBSTACLES

F r. Riehle's favorite job at Notre Dame may have been serving as the athletic department's sports chaplain but his most important contribution to students, professors, administrators and others could have been his critical role there as the head of discipline during the Vietnam War era. Even though the latter duty is one that he disliked, Fr. Riehle earned accolades for performing that job well. Indeed, he defused potentially violent and destructive protests when many other campuses at the time became chaotic scenes of uncontrolled student unrest.

Fr. Riehle met directly with protestors at Notre Dame. He once saved the ROTC building on Notre Dame's campus from succumbing to the plans of certain students who plotted to set it on fire with the intent of burning it to the ground. In that instance, he recruited others to help him cool off the protestors. The protests posed obstacles for Fr. Riehle but they did not prove to be insurmountable with the right responses.

Fr. Riehle became a proactive dean of students in 1967 at Notre Dame during a contentious era on college campuses across the country. Passionate student protests proliferated, the Vietnam War raged and young men worried that a compulsory military draft reinstituted during December 1969 soon would send them from the classroom into the battle fields of Southeast Asia. President Richard Nixon sparked further unrest when he announced on April 30, 1970, that U.S. forces had entered into Cambodia.

But at Notre Dame, Fr. Riehle earned respect from students and administrators alike for helping to carry out Fr. Theodore Hesburgh's directive of maintaining a learning atmosphere at Notre Dame, while allowing freedom of expression without campus-wide chaos.

Fr. Riehle's pre-seminary background as a salesman proved useful when he needed to persuade students to accept the university's policies or at least obey them. It was not a period of time when conforming to the wishes of people in authority was done without question. Fr. Riehle willingly talked to students himself to address their concerns directly. The dialogue proved to be important in keeping the campus relatively calm, compared to others around the country.

Indefatigable Defender

Fr. Riehle's intervention helped immensely during the student revolution of the 1960s, amid the Vietnam War protests when the presidents of 250 universities, including those at all of the Ivy League schools, lost their jobs, former Notre Dame President Theodore Hesburgh recalled.

When campuses around the country were "falling apart," Fr. Riehle exerted discipline and enforced behavioral standards at Notre Dame that prevented the situation there from exploding out of control, Fr Hesburgh added.

"Students could protest, but needed to do so peacefully, and not infringe on the rights of other students," Fr. Hesburgh said.

During one potentially volatile encounter with student protestors, Fr. Riehle met with those who were lying in front of the door of a campus building to block the entrance and reminded the students they were attending school at a "special" place, Fr. Hesburgh recalled.

"Jim simply told them, 'You have 10 minutes to cease and desist; If you are still here when I come back, I will have to pick up the duties that I don't like very much but which I must do.' And, he picked up all of their ID cards and left. I think he gave them a little longer than 10 minutes but when he came back, they were all there lying on the floor in front of the recruiting office."

Fr. Riehle spoke clearly and forcefully when he faced them the second time.

Warnings Carried Weight

"Gentlemen, you've had your warning," Fr. Riehle said. He told them all that they were expelled and needed to be off the campus by noon. If they did not leave the front of the building within the next 10 minutes, they would no longer be Notre Dame students ever again.

When he returned, they had left but gone directly to the office of Fr. Hesburgh, who heard them complain about Fr. Riehle's unyielding words and threats of expulsion.

"You can't stand behind Jim Riehle and this decision," the students protested.

"I said, 'Fr. Jim is doing a difficult thing. None of us enjoy this kind of thing. You had your chance; you blew it. You will all be off this campus by noon,'" Fr. Hesburgh said. "But we're not just cutting you loose forever. All of you can come back and begin the next semester and all is forgiven.'"

That situation showed Fr. Riehle's value as the university's dean of students during tumultuous times, Fr. Hesburgh said.

"This is one of the few universities in the land, thanks to Jim's firm hand and steady discipline, where the people who tried to do something outrageous were stopped," Fr. Hesburgh said.

Baptism by Fire

Such an instance occurred one morning at 5 a.m. when protestors arrived in front of the ROTC building on campus with buckets of fire in one hand and buckets of gasoline in the other, Fr. Hesburgh said. Fr Riehle was ready for them. He knew the tactics of war and had arranged for other students to double-team each protestor, with each interceptor able to take one bucket apiece, dump the fire and gasoline in a nearby lake and end the potential threat of having a building set on fire. In addition, the hot-headed students were cooled off unceremoniously as the arms and legs of each were grabbed and the fire-burning dissenters were flung into the "cold April water of St. Mary's Lake," Fr. Hesburgh said.

It is not a dip that most people would take on their own. The response may have been a "bit macho," Fr. Hesburgh conceded during his eulogy of Fr. Riehle, but the results were effective.

"It saved the day," Fr. Hesburgh said. "It saved the building and it maintained the peace, as it was maintained on very few campuses at that time."

Tenacious Toughness

"You can talk about his message every Saturday in the pre-game Mass," former football coach Bob Davie said. But what stands out most about Fr. Riehle, Davie said, is the way that he persevered when various health problems afflicted him during the nine years that the coach worked with the chaplain at Notre Dame.

"I think the most inspirational thing was just his toughness," Davie said. As diabetes limited Fr. Riehle's mobility, he still found ways to use golf carts or whatever else was necessary to perform his duties as the team chaplain.

"He really had problems walking and getting around at different stages," Davie said. "He would find a way to make it to every Friday Quarterback Club luncheon."

The coach and chaplain would sit together on the dais at each one of the luncheons, no matter what ailment had befallen the elderly priest most recently, Davie said. The clergyman's fortitude impressed the football coach.

"He would find a way to make it to every away game," Davie said. "He would be on the sidelines."

The chaplain showed courage in serving in his later years, despite his declining health, Davie said. No matter how infirmed the priest might appear, he somehow mustered up the strength to give a stirring homily at the pre-game Mass that bordered on a "pep rally," Davie recalled.

"There was no question who he wanted to see win the game," Davie said. Fr. Riehle seemed to find an inner strength to deliver rousing remarks whenever he addressed the team at a pre-game Mass or delivered an invocation to the thousands of fans who might attend a Quarterback Club luncheon, Davie recalled.

No-Excuses Nurse

Mary Pat Russ, Fr. Riehle's nurse at the Holy Cross House that served as the on-campus home for elderly priests, would not relent when Fr. Riehle grumbled about doing physical therapy or anything else as his diabetes condition worsened.

"She would put him in his place," said Jim Fraleigh, a deputy athletic director at Notre Dame. If Fr. Riehle complained about doing any exercise, she insisted that he forge ahead.

"I'm convinced it extended his life," said Fraleigh, who recalled telling Fr. Riehle as much. In response, the priest flashed a "weird smile," as if to acknowledge the statement's truth without admitting it, Fraleigh recalled.

Infernal Infirmities

Fr. Riehle's debilitating diabetes limited his athletic lifestyle and activities dramatically, as well as subdued his personality "a little bit," said former athletic trainer John Whitmer.

"He became a little bit more sullen because a great part of his tenure at the university was being a part of athletics," Whitmer said. In his heyday, Fr. Riehle loved to travel as a chaplain with the football, hockey and basketball teams.

Ultimately, Fr. Riehle needed to leave traveling with the teams to others, as well as give up "adult beverages" and stop smoking cigars, Whitmer said.

Fr. Riehle had no choice but to give up activities that he loved as his body failed.

"As time unfolded and Jim became less able to do things physically, then we tried to accommodate his limitations and take advantage of his great relationships with so many former athletes," former President Fr. Edward "Monk" Malloy said.

Walked the Walk

The way that Fr. Riehle guided others to live their lives was just how he lived his own, Davie said. No one needed to look any further than Fr. Riehle himself for an example of his values because he exhibited them each day, Davie added.

"He is probably the thing I miss most about Notre Dame—just standing next to him on the sideline," Davie said.

The chaplain's commitment went beyond the team's success and extended to looking out for the well-being of the coaches and the players, Davie recalled.

"I'm not Catholic," said Davie, a Presbyterian. "That didn't have anything to do with it."

Accepting Pain

Unlike most of his teammates who arrived together as freshmen on football scholarships, former defensive lineman Tom "Big T" Ross sustained career-ending injuries while at Notre Dame that prevented him from playing in a varsity game.

"After multiple back surgeries at Notre Dame as a result of my football injuries, there were days when I could barely walk," said Ross, who acknowledged that he has felt pain every day since then. "But I never complained and still don't. Look around; you'll always find someone who's got it worse than you."

His former teammate Ed "Duke" Scales, who played linebacker for the Fighting Irish, stayed in close contact with Ross after they graduated. Sympathetic to his buddy's plight, Scales felt regret that his pal never enjoyed the pleasure of playing on the 1973 national championship team or receiving a varsity letter that would have entitled him to membership in Notre Dame's Monogram Club and full-fledged participation in its activities.

"He [Duke] thought I 'earned' my monogram by giving up my health," Ross said. "I did not agree and I stayed clear of Monogram [Club] activities."

Spouse's Subterfuge

Fr. Riehle played a key role in surprising Ross with an honorary monogram in 1999. But it took much effort, planning and subterfuge by a number of people to make the special night possible.

Despite Ross insisting he was unworthy of a monogram, his pal Duke Scales knew the sacrifices endured by his former teammate as well as anyone and pursued the honor for his friend behind the scenes.

The 1999 Monogram Club banquet marked the 25th anniversary of the class of 1974, so a special reunion was planned that weekend. Ross intended to attend the weekend's reunion, but not the Monogram Club banquet on Thursday evening. His friend Scales, however, urged Ross to join him at the banquet.

"I was working in Milwaukee that week and couldn't attend, lest I get fired," Ross said. "Unbeknownst to me, my wife, Jan, called my boss and explained that I was to receive a surprise, honorary monogram at that banquet and she asked that the company let me attend."

One Last Hurrah?

Aside from seeking and receiving approval from Ross's employer for him to attend the banquet, his wife also needed to concoct a story to convince her husband that he had to be there. Her ruse required explaining that his best friend Scales was "very ill." She said it could be Scales's last chance to attend a Monogram Club banquet and that her husband had "better be there," Ross recalled.

"Remember, I did not know what everyone was planning that night," Ross said. "My boss called me and said 'take off,' so I drove to Notre Dame and made it in time. I was completely surprised when they called Duke to the podium and he announced me as an honorary recipient. All of my Notre Dame buddies were in attendance and I was thoroughly appreciative but unworthy of such an honor. I was, and still am, completely humbled by the experience. I found out after the fact that Duke had to jump through many hoops to get me that monogram... a better friend hath no man than to stick out his neck for a buddy."

Duke Scales recalled needing to meet the "by-the-book" requirements of Fr. Riehle to gather and to submit letters of recommendation from other Monogram Club members. He also wrote one himself to attest to Ross's "character" and to support giving him an honorary letter.

"I had to lie like hell," Scales joked about the letter he wrote. In the days when Notre Dame was an all-male institution, poking fun at each other to get a laugh became an art form.

In a serious moment, Scales explained that Fr. Riehle was among those who recognized Ross's dedication and knew that the honor was deserved. After all, Fr. Riehle had been the football team's chaplain during Ross's injury-shortened football career. The priest never opposed the nomination of Ross for the honor, Scales confirmed.

"He just wanted all the I's dotted & T's crossed because that was his way," Scales said.

Windy City Road Trip

On another occasion, Marty Gleason, an organizer with the Notre Dame Club of Chicago, contacted Fr. Riehle to enlist the chaplain's help to invite football coaches and players to attend an event. The Chicago club planned to celebrate the team's national championship just weeks after a dominating 38-10 New Year's Day Cotton Bowl victory in 1978 against then-No. 1 ranked University of Texas. Head Coach Dan Devine initially declined the invitation due to a scheduling conflict but Fr. Riehle turned the event into a great success by filling a couple of buses with coaches and players. After Joe Montana, the team's star quarterback, Digger Phelps, the basketball coach, and many others committed to attend, Devine rearranged his schedule to join them, Gleason said.

"If we ever needed any help with anything, he [Fr. Riehle] always delivered," Gleason said. "He always showed up for our events."

Fr. Riehle was a regular attendee of the Chicago-based Notre Dame Club's annual "Knute Rockne Dinner," Gleason said. The dinner, named after the university's original legendary football coach, was one of the club's biggest annual activities.

"I knew about Rockne before I knew about God or Notre Dame," Gleason said.

Backup Ballplayer

As a Notre Dame quarterback who was on the back end of the team's depth chart when he started his college career, Montana recalled turning to Fr. Riehle for guidance numerous times. Before Montana became the team's starting quarterback, he often heard encouraging words from Fr. Riehle when disappointments arose. Montana's first dose of reality was arriving at Notre Dame and discovering seven other freshmen quarterbacks ready to compete with him.

"I'm sure my first couple years weren't very productive," Montana said. "I know I spent a lot of time talking to him. I'm sure a lot of it was really more along the lines of confidence and making sure you stay focused on what you are doing."

Poise under pressure became a hallmark for Montana as a collegian and later in the National Football League. Montana led Notre Dame to seven come-from-behind victories, including two wins after entering the games in relief as a sophomore in 1975. After missing the 1976 season with a separated shoulder, Montana returned as a redshirt junior in 1977 and led the Fighting Irish to the national championship.

Montana was no exception among the Notre Dame players who gravitated toward Fr. Riehle.

"I think he was there for everybody, just trying to make people understand that it's a game and you're going to have your ups and downs," Montana said. "It's not always easy. He'd help you learn to fight through it."

Although no particular moment with Fr. Riehle stands out, what is most memorable is the priest's accessibility, Montana said.

"He was always around," Montana said. "He was the eternal optimist for all of us. He was like a coach, I guess you could say, because he lived with our ups and downs."

Despite Montana leading Notre Dame to a national championship, he also endured setbacks on his journey to stardom. Fr. Riehle listened and offered advice when Montana or others sought him out for help through a difficult time.

"When I was down, he was down," Montana said. "But he also was there trying help get you back up on your feet again. When the highs were high, he was up there with us, laughing and joking. Just like he did in the commercial, he was always joking about somebody or something."

Comeback Kid

As for Montana, he developed a knack for rallying his team to victory at Notre Dame that carried into professional football. At Notre Dame, Montana gained a national reputation for calmly leading fourth-quarter comebacks. Fr. Riehle was an unshakable symbol of faith during each game and his presence certainly did not go unnoticed on the sidelines. The chaplain personified quiet strength under pressure.

"One of the things that I've learned over the years was to try to be the same at the beginning of the game, as much as I was at the end of the game," Montana said. "I tried to be the same throughout, up or down. Until the game was over, you always believed that you could win."

Montana then laughed and acknowledged, "In some cases you were crazy." The score was just too lopsided to overcome but an athlete never wants to admit that to himself. Instead, the ideal attitude should be to maintain a can-do spirit, regardless of the odds, he added.

"We tried to go back to fundamentals and do things that would get us back on track," Montana said.

Fourth-quarter comebacks also may indicate something other than valor under fire, Montana explained.

"You played crappy enough to get you in that position," Montana said with a laugh, "so that you had to come back, but you still had the wherewithal to go ahead and make that happen."

Hard-earned Humility

Montana said his first college and professional football games turned into disasters. In college, he remembered an inauspicious start against the University of Michigan.

"We played their freshmen team," Montana said. "I think I had a couple of interceptions."

The experience lets Montana offer sage advice to others about persevering in the face of adversity, as Fr. Riehle counseled.

"I keep telling my boys, you can't do any worse than my start in college," Montana said.

Despite winning four Super Bowl titles, Montana also had a rough initiation into the NFL.

"In my first start against Seattle, I had two interceptions run back for touchdowns," Montana said. "A guy had the nerve to run me over on the one-yard line on the second touchdown. Those are the kind of things that happen to you. But the only place to go from there is up."

The national championship at Notre Dame, the four Super Bowls wins with the San Francisco 49ers and his induction into the NFL Hall of Fame show that Montana rebounded well from all of his early disappointments.

"The guys I played with made that happen and I was just fortunate to be with them," Montana said.

Chicken Soup for 'the Throw'

Montana played in the 1979 Cotton Bowl while ailing from the flu during his senior year and suffered from hypothermia during a game that was played in freezing temperatures against the University of Houston. At halftime, Dr. Leslie Bodnar, Notre Dame's orthopedic specialist, and Dr. John Thompson, the team's physician, treated Montana. In addition, Fr. Riehle gave his customary blessing to the players before they took the field. Montana, who was shivering uncontrollably, received special attention from the physicians, who decided that a packet of instant chicken soup powder that they brought with them might be just what the quarterback needed on an unseasonably cold, icy and windy New Year's Day in Dallas, Texas.

The chicken soup was "nice and hot," former athletic trainer John Whitmer recalled.

After trying other ways to warm the chilled quarterback that did little good, Dr. Bodnar spoon-fed the soup to Montana during halftime. Dr. Thompson stayed with Montana while the rest of the team returned to the field with Fr. Riehle to begin the second half. The chicken soup seemed to "serve its purpose" by offering a much-needed medicinal benefit, Whitmer said.

Montana returned to the field late in the third quarter to brave the frigid conditions and he played the rest of the game. Whether it was the chicken soup, Fr. Riehle's blessing or a combination of factors that helped put Montana back onto the playing field, Notre Dame began an improbable 22-point, fourth quarter comeback against Houston. Possibly the greatest come-from-behind victory in Cotton Bowl history culminated with an 8-yard touchdown pass from Montana to David "Kris" Haines with no time left on the game clock to give Notre Dame a 35-34 win.

That touchdown pass is the one mentioned by Fr. Riehle as "one great throw" during a television commercial for Adidas shoes that he taped with Montana years later.

Harsh Holiday with Houston

The 1979 Cotton Bowl in Houston was the last collegiate game for Montana and Haines as they joined their teammates, coaches and Fr. Riehle in enduring some of the harshest weather in the history of college football bowl games.

"Two years in a row, I came down with a virus," said Haines, who recalled feeling too ill to practice for two or three days before playing in the Cotton Bowl on a frigid New Year's Day with a wind chill of minus 7 degrees Fahrenheit.

The weather was so cold, windy and icy on the morning of the scheduled contest that Haines was among the players who asked team officials if the game might be canceled or postponed.

"I felt horrible," Haines said.

At that point, Haines said he had "no idea" whether he might play any football games in the future. He ultimately became a wide receiver for the Chicago Bears in the NFL between 1979 and 1981 but he could not remember any game played in worse conditions than the 1979 Cotton Bowl against the University of Houston. ESPN ranked that game in a 2008 feature as one of the top cold weather sporting events in modern history.

Edward "Moose" Krause, the late Notre Dame athletic director, called the Fighting Irish's win that day the greatest comeback in the team's history.

Haines still remembers the day more than 35 years later and recalls seeing Fr. Riehle standing on the sidelines "freezing" with everyone else.

"He looked cold but it didn't look like he was as cold as everybody else," Haines said about the Michigan native who grew up skating and playing hockey outdoors during the long winters of the Great Lakes State.

Display Dedication

Fr. Riehle also was a fixture in Joe Theismann's career at Notre Dame before the quarterback later won a Super Bowl in the NFL. The priest joined the team for breakfast, practice, the games and the Masses. He set a tone of dedication and determination, Theismann said.

"I was one of 13 quarterbacks," Theismann said. "I wasn't a good student. I went out on two dates my first two years in college. My whole world was wrapped up in academics, trying to stay eligible, and football."

Theismann said he tried to live up to Fr. Riehle's expectations to exert the effort required of a Notre Dame student.

Occasionally, Theismann would play pool or basketball for recreation but those were exceptions to his devotion to school and football.

"He brought great counsel to young men," Theismann said.

Inauspicious Entrance

When playing the University of Southern California (USC) in a traditional late season matchup during his sophomore year in 1968, Theismann recalled throwing an interception in his first pass of the game that was picked off along the right sideline by USC defensive back Sandy Durko, who raced into the Notre Dame end zone 21 yards away for a touchdown.

"I remember throwing it," Theismann said. "I remember watching him run in the end zone. I remember jogging toward the sidelines."

The first face Theismann noticed as he headed toward the sideline belonged to Fr. Riehle.

"There was this look of calm," Theismann said. "He looked at me like, 'Don't worry about it, it's going to be okay.'"

Theismann then walked by his coach, Ara Parseghian.

Confident Quarterback

"I said to Ara, 'Don't worry about it, I'll get it back,'" said Theismann, who added that at that moment Fr. Riehle's confidence seemed to be transferred to him through a single glance.

Theismann backed up his promise by guiding Notre Dame to score three unanswered touchdowns in staking the Fighting Irish to a 21-7 halftime lead.

"So, I got that one back and two extra," Theismann said with a laugh. Theismann's assurance that he would overcome the mistake put the coach's mind at ease. At that pivotal moment, Parseghian learned that his quarterback would not be rattled by "interceptions or things that went bad during a game," Theismann said the coach later told him.

USC rallied to tie the game and it finished that way in an era before modern day overtime rules would have produced a winner one way or another. The game also featured USC running back O.J. Simpson as a Heisman Trophy candidate during his senior year.

"The three years that I played USC, they tied us twice and we lost once," Theismann said.

Grins and Glances

One of the ways that Fr. Riehle expressed himself was through a "little grin," Theismann said.

"It seemed like everybody had this look back then… a look of acknowledgement, a look of appreciation, a quizzical look," Theismann said. "I don't know whether he [Fr. Riehle] picked it up from Ara [Parseghian] or what but it seemed like the two of them had a similar quality."

All Fr. Riehle or Coach Parseghian had to do was give you a glance to communicate a message, Theismann said.

"You could look at him and see a quiet strength," Theismann said. "You could look at him and see a quizzical nature, like, 'What are you doing?'"

Parseghian's Partner

Ara Parseghian was the one who set the tone of never having a breaking point and Fr. Riehle helped to emphasize it, Theismann said.

"As Fr. Riehle did God's work, he also did Ara's," Theismann said. "And I guarantee you that there were times when I couldn't tell the difference between the two of them."

One of Joe Theismann's teammates on the football squad was a walk-on player named Peter Schivarelli, who became the manager of the Chicago rock band. The stereotypical portrayal of a rock star in the media is someone who has been arrested 12 times, said Schivarelli, who earned a roster spot after Coach Parseghian agreed to give him a chance. Schivarelli ran afoul of Fr. Riehle when the priest was the dean of students but grew to respect and admire the clergyman, before joining Chicago in the music business.

"We don't fit the actual mold of a rock band," Schivarelli said.

When asked how members of his band differ from other musicians, Schivarelli characterized them as "boring guys" who play "tremendous" music. Proof of the latter capability has been borne out by the band garnering dozens of gold albums. A gold album requires notching sales of 1 million copies, while a platinum album is earned with sales of 2 million copies.

Schivarelli overcame long odds to gain admission to Notre Dame, made the football team as a non-scholarship player and ended up managing one of the most successful rock bands in music history. Generous contributions to the university and to various charities since his graduation helped to distance Schivarelli from the unflattering impression he made as a rules-breaking freshman when he first crossed paths with Fr. Riehle.

Notre Dame or Bust

"For me, I came out of high school and I had scholarship offers," Schivarelli said.

But none of the offers came from Notre Dame, Schivarelli's Holy Grail.

"There was a great high school team and they took four players from that one team in Chicago," Schivarelli said.

Since Notre Dame recruited nationally, it was not going to offer football scholarships to "ten guys" from the Windy City, Schivarelli said.

"For me, the only place I ever wanted to go was Notre Dame," Schivarelli said. Rather than attend another college, Schivarelli opted to begin working to earn a living. No one in Schivarelli's family ever had pursued a formal education beyond high school.

Trailblazer for 'Rudy'

"Rudy went to Notre Dame after I did," Schivarelli said. "Even he said, when I met him, a lot of ideas he got were from hearing stories about me being there."

Similar to Rudy, Schivarelli hailed from a working-class family in the Midwest and achieved his long-shot goal of playing football at Notre Dame during Fr. Riehle's tenure as the seemingly ever-present team chaplain.

Former Notre Dame Assistant Football Coach George Kelly is credited with calling Schivarelli the "real Rudy." Joe Theismann, who quarterbacked Notre Dame and played four seasons of football there with Schivarelli also began using the same nickname for his former teammate, once the movie *Rudy* gained acclaim.

But Schivarelli unfortunately made a negative early impression on Fr. Riehle by bringing a car onto campus as a freshman in violation of the university's rules at the time.

Last-Chance Chaplain

An all-male school when Schivarelli attended Notre Dame, the university's rules, regulations and restrictions left little room for interpretation. Any infraction—even seemingly small ones—could result in needing to appear before Fr. Riehle for judgment. Christians who believe in everlasting life expect a pivotal day to account for their actions will come after one's earthly existence ends. For Notre Dame students at that time, Fr. Riehle gave them an introduction into what it might be like to face a final judgment. Back then, Fr. Riehle was a student's judge, jury and last hope for mercy.

Fr. Riehle's stint as dean of students from 1967 until 1973 required him to punish students who violated the rules and Schivarelli soon discovered that bringing a luxury car onto campus as a first semester freshman brought him directly into the disapproving sights of Fr. Riehle.

"He [Fr. Riehle] kept pursuing me for my car," Schivarelli said. "Of course, I'd have it at practice and I still was living on campus. He would come over and he'd have a fit."

The priest ultimately impounded Schivarelli's Cadillac convertible. At the time, only second-semester seniors could keep a vehicle on campus.

When Schivarelli explained he needed the car to return to Chicago on the weekends to earn money in the retail clothing business to fund his education, Fr. Riehle proposed his idea of a solution. Each time Schivarelli wanted to drive to Chicago on a weekend, the student needed to seek out Fr. Riehle to retrieve the keys.

"The car was critical to me," said Schivarelli, who added that he had a "good job" in Chicago that he needed to keep to pay his way through Notre Dame.

Buddy System

Frightened of the potential consequences of a repeat violation of campus rules, Schivarelli said he was too scared to approach the priest to ask for the use of his Cadillac until the end of the semester. Instead, Schivarelli had his friends bring another car from Chicago for him to drive. Schivarelli made a point of keeping that one off campus by parking it two blocks away— just to be sure he complied with the rules. The plan worked to perfection. Schivarelli remained a student and a football player at Notre Dame for four years until his graduation, as well as learned valuable lessons about persevering in the face of adversity.

A large part of Schivarelli's challenge in conforming to the rules for freshmen stemmed from the unconventional path that he took to enroll at Notre Dame, following three years of working after high school. Since the status symbol in Schivarelli's Italian neighborhood was one's automobile, he opted to seek the approval of his friends and neighbors by buying a prestigious car. Once he drove onto the Notre Dame campus with the seemingly ostentatious car that a typical college freshman could only dream of owning one day, he unwittingly projected a brazen image of himself to Fr. Riehle and others as a status-conscious student almost as soon as he arrived.

Schivarelli also drew suspicion to himself by engaging in an unusual extracurricular activity. As other freshmen focused on adapting to life at the academically rigorous school, he sold cut-rate merchandise to his fellow students out of the trunk of his vehicle. It took place during a time before the advent of outlet shopping malls.

"Fr. Jim wanted to catch him the whole time he was the dean of students but never did," Al Szewczyk said.

Since the car he used was no jalopy, it was not readily apparent to an onlooker that Schivarelli was in financial need. Despite coming to the university as a cash-strapped student who spent much of his savings on his

Cadillac, Schivarelli's use of a posh car and his oddly successful entrepreneurial endeavors reasonably could have given the impression to Fr. Riehle and other observers that he may have been selling goods procured from suppliers of questionable repute.

At best, it was far from exemplary behavior in the priest's eyes. For the early part of Schivarelli's years at Notre Dame, Fr. Riehle projected an intimidating presence and possessed fear-inducing power among the students as the university's disciplinarian. As much as Fr. Riehle disliked the duty, he proved adept at spurring compliance with campus rules, after giving stern warnings or sanctions to offending students. Schivarelli became a reluctant recipient of the priest's unabashed willingness to maintain behavioral standards at Notre Dame.

Fr. Riehle cast a giant shadow during Schivarelli's Notre Dame years and still exerted an influence on the former student long after graduation.

Fr. Riehle's Reprieve

An appreciation of Schivarelli's working-class background is important to understand how he ended up in his public-image predicament. As the first member of his family to attend college, Schivarelli triggered his father's ire by forgoing a paying job to attend Notre Dame and incurring considerable expense.

"The one thing my father vowed is that he'd never give me a dime," Schivarelli said. "He was furious that I went. In those days, I struggled. And, if it wasn't for Ara helping me and giving me the partial scholarship fairly early, I wonder how I even would have made it."

To Fr. Riehle's credit, he showed enough restraint to allow Schivarelli to stay at the university and to keep the spot he earned on the football team. But that compassion did not come without the priest also imposing his own form of tough love. Afraid of any further clashes with the priest, Schivarelli quickly displayed an ability to adapt that ultimately served him well in life.

Petrifying Priest

"For me, it was kind of a nightmare, in a way," said Schivarelli, reminiscing about his dilemma of trying to figure out how to keep working to pay his way through Notre Dame, without breaking the university's rules enforced by Fr. Riehle. Schivarelli cited Victor Hugo's 1862 novel *Les Misérables*, and explained that he felt a little like the character Jean Valjean, who was chased relentlessly by a policeman named Javert for stealing a loaf of bread. Even though Valjean was starving and needed food, he still broke the law that Javert was responsible for enforcing, similar to Schivarelli violating the rule that barred non-seniors from keeping a car on campus.

Schivarelli acknowledged that Fr. Riehle's pursuit and confiscation of his car, as well as the need to avoid repeating the violation with a backup vehicle, were "not as severe" as Valjean's flight from the law that included escaping from prison and hiding his previous identity to remain free. But to a 21-year-old freshman who was trying to play on the football team and pay his way through Notre Dame, Fr. Riehle's enforcement of the rules seemed almost as threatening as the determined pursuer Javert was to Valjean.

Tuition to attend Notre Dame for four years totaled $10,000 when Schivarelli studied there. At $1,250 a semester, the tuition posed a burden.

"That was a lot of money in those days," Schivarelli said.

In 2013-2014, tuition, room and board for a full school year at Notre Dame topped $57,000. To give back to the university, Schivarelli pays for a scholarship every year that goes to student-athletes who participate in under-funded sports.

The reason is that as much as he scrambled to find a way to cover his tuition at Notre Dame, Schivarelli said he would have been even further strapped without the financial assistance that he received as a student.

When writing checks four times a year to fund a scholarship, Schivarelli said he recalls the generous help that he obtained from others.

Statue for a Legend

The spearheading of an initiative to erect a statue to honor Parseghian was another philanthropic endeavor that Schivarelli carried out for his alma mater. Out of 200 potential photos that both the sculptor and Parseghian reviewed independently to choose the image for the statue, both men picked the same one. The photo showed the coach held triumphantly on the shoulders of Schivarelli and another player after Notre Dame won the 1971 Cotton Bowl in a major upset of the University of Texas Longhorns. Incredibly, the talented Texas team had not lost a game in the previous three years.

"Only at Notre Dame could a walk-on have his own statue with the head coach," Schivarelli said. "I always get a kick out of that."

Schivarelli also regards Parseghian as a "great humanitarian" for devoting himself later in life to raise money in a heartfelt quest to find a treatment for a fatal, neurodegenerative disease. Niemann-Pick Type C (NP-C) is a genetic, cholesterol storage disorder that primarily afflicts children and ends their lives before or during adolescence.

For that reason, Parseghian's legacy extends beyond his glory years as Notre Dame's football coach and his successful partnership with Fr. Riehle. The former coach took up a new mantle when he helped a fledgling charitable foundation aimed at fighting the devastating disease of NP-C.

The coach championed fundraising for the Ara Parseghian Medical Research Foundation www.parseghian.org in 1994 as a loving response to the shocking news that three of his grandchildren, Michael, Marcia and Christa, had been diagnosed with the disease. The foundation has raised more than $40 million to fund 300-plus research grants around the world with the aim of developing a treatment or a cure.

The disease ultimately claimed the lives of all three Parseghian grandchildren who had been afflicted. Michael Parseghian died in 1997 at age 9, while his sisters Christa Parseghian, 10, and Marcia Parseghian, 16, finished their battles in 2001 and 2005, respectively.

Although the loss of the three youngest Parseghian grandchildren to the disease was almost unbearable, Parseghian explained that it brought forth the "pure goodness" of the human spirit that has been expressed through innumerable cards, letters, prayers and donations.

Philanthropic Performances

Once viewed with suspicion by Fr. Riehle, Schivarelli, along with the Chicago band that he manages, is among the foundation's highest-profile backers. In an entertainment industry known more for self-aggrandizing addictions of nearly every kind than for philanthropy, the Chicago band not only played two benefit concerts to raise funds for the cause but also has contributed a portion of every ticket sold to the foundation since the mid-1990s. In 1996, the Chicago band began to donate 25 cents of every ticket it sold at all of its performances to help fund medical research to fight the disease. The band's per-ticket contribution subsequently has doubled to 50 cents.

The first benefit concert occurred on campus at the indoor Joyce Center in South Bend after the 1995 Notre Dame-University of Texas football game. On that day, the Fighting Irish routed the Longhorns, 55-27. The game served as the unofficial opening act for a concert. The band's post-game concert raised more than $100,000 to give a huge boost to the fledgling initiative to fund research to combat the disease. It turned out to be far from a one-time contribution.

The Chicago band's second benefit concert took place in 2001 at a gala called "One More Victory, Ara!" The gala combined with an annual golf tournament to raise funds for the foundation. The band's philanthropic efforts on behalf of the charity have generated more than $1.2 million from ticket sales alone.

"Peter and Chicago have been tremendous supporters of our efforts," said Cindy Parseghian, president of the Ara Parseghian Medical Research Foundation.

The Schivarelli-led band also aids other charities. While 50 cents of each Chicago concert ticket goes to the Parseghian Foundation, another 50 cents of each ticket sold is donated to a charity called Hannah and Friends. The latter organization, founded by former Notre Dame football coach Charlie Weis, is named after his daughter, who has a seizure disorder (electrical status epilepticus of slow-wave sleep). The mission of Hannah and Friends is to improve the quality of life for children and adults with special needs. The charity's biggest project is to develop a 40-acre property to create a supportive community for the people it serves. The first house to accept live-in residents opened to four women on September 28, 2009. Called the "Peter Schivarelli and Chicago Home," its construction was funded entirely by donations from the band and its manager.

One of Schivarelli's greatest accomplishments may have been when the hard-to-please Fr. Riehle finally described him as a "good guy." It required patience for Schivarelli to hear those words, since he had graduated from Notre Dame years earlier. But Schivarelli appreciates the significance of redeeming himself in Fr. Riehle's eyes, unlike Jean Valjean, who never managed to reconcile with Javert in Victor Hugo's classic *Les Misérables*.

Verbal Butt-Kicking

"As a priest, Fr. Riehle was a character," Schivarelli said. "If Fr. Riehle felt that you needed it, he wanted to try to kick you in the ass."

Fr. Riehle could scare students with his demeanor but Schivarelli said he learned the priest was like a demanding coach who might yell to spur someone to improve.

"The first time I ever heard a priest swear, it was Fr. Riehle," Schivarelli said.

"I used to be as scared as I could be," Schivarelli said. But by his junior year, Schivarelli said Fr. Riehle "really understood" the Chicagoan's financial circumstances and need to earn money to pay for school.

The people at Notre Dame know "just about everything" a student does, Schivarelli said. Once he reached his junior year, Fr. Riehle realized Schivarelli worked hard in class and in football and was not "some kind of a wild man," he added.

"He was a gruff guy in a friendly way," said Schivarelli, who also described Fr. Riehle as "unique and down to Earth."

Accepting Challenges

Fr. Edmund Joyce and then-Notre Dame Athletic Director "Moose" Krause recruited Charles "Lefty" Smith to come to the university to start a varsity hockey program. At the time, Notre Dame only fielded a club hockey team but strong interest existed in upgrading it into an intercollegiate sport.

Accompanied by his assistant coach Tim McNeil, Smith arrived in South Bend, Indiana, and found no youth or high school hockey in the area. Other than about 20 Notre Dame students who played club hockey and arranged their own games against other teams, there was no hockey community in South Bend, Smith recalled. That deep void was daunting. But Smith found a loyal and supportive friend in the person of Fr. Riehle.

To spur interest in Notre Dame hockey, Smith and McNeil helped to develop youth hockey programs in the area. For example, Smith spearheaded the launch of the Irish Youth Hockey league in 1968, as well as a high school league within the community.

Tenacity Talks

Fr. Riehle was known to display admiration for people who kept giving their best efforts in the face of adversity. One recollection in particular that illustrated his love of a fighting spirit for those who persevere in sports is reflected in the following story.

"In 1983, as the Notre Dame varsity hockey program was being terminated, the team had a late season series at Western Michigan, and I happened to be there for the final regular season game," said Professor John Gaski, who had returned to Notre Dame in 1980 as a new faculty member after earning a Ph.D. from the University of Wisconsin. "Our guys came back with three goals in the last two minutes to win the game. When I encountered Fr. Riehle a few minutes later, his comment was, 'Do these guys have balls or what?'"

The players knew the team would be eliminated and battled to the very end—earning the frankly spoken praise from Fr. Riehle.

Smith remembered that game and the grit of his players, too.

"We won the Great Lakes Championship in 1983 and were informed that we would be dropping out of the League, and guys on scholarship would maintain them until they graduated, but no new scholarships would be given," Smith said.

Naturally, Smith, as the university's founding varsity hockey coach, described it as a "horrible decision." University officials who ultimately restored offering hockey scholarships have been vindicated by the team's success. The team now contends regularly for the NCAA "Frozen Four" in which four regional champions play for a national title, just as the NCAA Basketball Tournament features its regional winners in a "Final Four." Notre Dame reached college hockey's "Frozen Four" in both 2008 and 2011.

Smith recalled the university dropped the sport in '83, brought it back as a club sport for a few years and then operated as a varsity non-scholarship sport. The university later offered limited scholarships and finally returned to giving scholarships in the mid '90s.

Showing His Teeth

The story about how Fr. Riehle helped Dr. Steven Gorman overcome living on welfare as the son of two high-school dropouts to become a cosmetic dentist may be one of the best examples of how the priest's gruff exterior hid a tender heart. The priest played a pivotal role in keeping Dr. Gorman at Notre Dame when it appeared financial barriers would pose too high of a hurdle. Rather than allow finances to force a dedicated student out of the university, Fr. Riehle intervened and turned it into a personal mission to help Dr. Gorman continue his education there.

Dr. Gorman, who earned his Bachelor of Arts degree from Notre Dame in 1977, now practices dentistry in his home state of Minnesota. He has pursued post-graduate training with aesthetic-dentistry trendsetters nationwide. From his humble background, no such professional prominence seemed likely. Dr. Gorman established his dental practice in the Twin Cities suburb of North Oaks, Minnesota, where he and his wife, Connie, chose to raise their three children, Emily, Anna and Madeline. Their oldest daughter, Emily, followed her father to Notre Dame and ended up living in Pangborn Hall, where her dad resided for his first three years at the university. Dr. Gorman attended Notre Dame starting as a freshman in 1973, one year after female undergraduates first gained admission. Pangborn Hall became an all-female dorm in 1992.

Elusive Quest

The complete impact of Fr. Riehle's role in helping Dr. Gorman fulfill his dream of graduating from Notre Dame cannot be appreciated fully without describing how the future dentist persevered amid limited financial resources and an unstable home life. His parents moved the family repeatedly in an elusive quest to improve their living situation. The dentist's father, Edward Gorman, hailed from Minnesota, while Dr. Gorman's mother, Ruby (Hall) Gorman, was raised on a cotton farm in Alabama as one of 12 children in her family. His parents met in Alabama while his dad was stationed there, after he enlisted in the Army in the early 1950s during the Korean conflict.

When Dr. Gorman's parents married, they moved to Minnesota where his father tried to earn a living as a truck driver. His dad's job prospects were hampered by a limited education that ended in the eighth grade. At the age of 3, Dr. Gorman and his family moved back to Alabama. In Mobile, Alabama, he learned to play baseball and other sports. Just prior to the start of the eighth grade, Dr. Gorman's family, including a sister who was two years younger and a one-year-old brother who was 12 years his junior, moved back to Minnesota. Roughly 18 months later, his parents divorced.

Absentee Father

"My dad kind of disappeared and I lost track of him for a few years," Dr. Gorman said.

Health problems prevented Dr. Gorman's mother from working for a period of time, leaving the family financially strapped. They relied on food stamps and other public assistance to survive.

As the oldest child, Dr. Gorman shopped for the family when his mother was ailing. Recollections of personally using food stamps for the family left an indelible impression on him. The experience reinforced Dr. Gorman's interest as a youngster in focusing on education to develop the kind of career opportunities unavailable to his parents.

"I always did well in school and I had good people encouraging me," including teachers, Dr. Gorman said.

In high school, Dr. Gorman played baseball, football and basketball. His contact with adult mentors outside of his family built his interest in attending college. The road to Notre Dame at that point seemed untenable. At that stage, Dr. Gorman had no expectation of ever attending school there. However, he steadfastly pursued his education.

Influential Coaches

"I had some good influences among my coaches, for sure," Dr. Gorman said.

As he entered his senior year in high school, Dr. Gorman was looking forward to the start of football season when his mother remarried and moved to Pennsylvania, before later going to Ohio. Not wanting to miss spending his senior year of high school with his friends, Dr. Gorman arranged to stay in Minnesota and to live with a pal and his family for the fall semester.

"The only problem with that is that they had a family of five and a two-bedroom duplex," Dr. Gorman said with a laugh. Dr. Gorman lived in the basement with one of the family's sons.

A high school girlfriend led Dr. Gorman to his next home when she introduced him to Dave Metzen, an elementary school principal who also was a graduate student of education at the University of Minnesota. Metzen and his wife, Leslie, a law school student at night who taught high school Spanish during the day, invited the high school senior to live with them in exchange for doing work around their house. He moved into the Metzen's home after Christmas of his final year of high school.

"They didn't have any kids, had been married a year or a year-and-a-half, and they found out about my living situation," Dr. Gorman remembered.

The arrangement clicked and living with two educators further propelled Dr. Gorman toward attending college. Ultimately, Metzen and his wife became "a second family" to him, Dr. Gorman recalled.

Metzen the Mentor

Even though Metzen never studied at Notre Dame, he proved to be instrumental in Dr. Gorman attending the school and meeting Fr. Riehle. Metzen had played hockey at South St. Paul High School, where "Lefty" Smith served as the hockey coach prior to leaving to become the first varsity hockey coach at Notre Dame. Metzen played college hockey at the University of Minnesota, which is a traditional power in the sport.

"I ended up going down to visit Notre Dame with a couple of friends of mine who were being recruited to play hockey there," Dr. Gorman recalled. "There were a couple of other kids from the St. Paul area who were on the same trip."

None of the other four students on the trip enrolled at Notre Dame, but Dr. Gorman said he "really liked the place" and chose to seek admission.

"The funny story is the day we were there, Lefty turned to my two friends and me from my high school and said, 'I don't see your SAT scores.' None of us had taken it," Dr. Gorman recalled.

As they spoke on a Friday night, Coach Smith mentioned that the SAT would be given on campus the following morning and he urged the students who were visiting him to take it. Despite needing to do so without any preparation, Dr. Gorman recalled scoring well enough to gain admission to Notre Dame. However, he lacked the financial means to attend the elite Catholic university.

Financial Follies

"My stepfather at the time stated that he was going to help me and that college funding would not be a problem," Dr. Gorman said. "I applied for some financial aid but I wasn't too concerned about it."

At the time, Notre Dame's annual tuition totaled $4,300, Dr. Gorman recalled. His stepfather made the first down payment of $600.

"That was the last money that I received from him," Dr. Gorman said.

Smith arranged for his son Mike to become Dr. Gorman's roommate during their freshmen year. They were assigned to Pangborn Hall, where Fr. Riehle served as the rector. At the time, Notre Dame only admitted male students and the dormitory was filled with a number of athletes from the football, basketball and hockey teams.

Road Less Traveled

It is almost a rite of passage in America for parents to chauffer their sons and daughters to college but Dr. Gorman took the proverbial road less traveled by arranging his own transportation to begin his freshman year at Notre Dame.

"I drove there myself and had all my stuff in a U-Haul," Dr. Gorman said. "Lefty's son Mike was there and helped me to unload my stuff."

Dr. Gorman also met Fr. Riehle shortly after he arrived on campus as a new student. As the dorm's rector, the priest lived in the residence hall and his room was only about four or five doors away from the one that Dr. Gorman and his roommate shared. The group of rooms directly down the hall from Fr. Riehle became known as "rector's row." Usually, the students on that floor are relocated after their freshmen year. However, Fr. Riehle enjoyed the camaraderie with the students on rector's row so much that he reportedly asked to keep the band of brothers intact as long as the men lived on campus during their time at Notre Dame. Despite the priest's characteristically tough-guy facade, the students who became acquainted with him realized that he offered something more valuable than style points that often took the form of sage advice.

Zamboni Man

To help pay his bills throughout college, Dr. Gorman held two jobs while studying at Notre Dame. One involved working for Smith and driving the Zamboni machine that resurfaced the campus ice rink, which the hockey coach supervised as a second job of his own. Dr. Gorman's other job could be described as somewhat of a sweet assignment, since he worked at the dormitory's dining hall on the dessert line.

"I did both jobs for four years," Dr. Gorman said.

The campus golf course was directly behind the dormitory and an ideal location for an avid golfer such as Fr. Riehle.

Without realizing it at the time, Dr. Gorman had a pair of sometimes grouchy guardian angels looking after him in the persons of Fr. Riehle and Smith.

The close friendship between Fr. Riehle and Smith let the hockey coach check on his son's roommate through the eyes and ears of the vigilant rector.

"A lot of times, I didn't even know it was going on," said Dr. Gorman, who later surmised that he had a good network of people looking after him at Notre Dame.

Sweltering Work

After freshman year, Dr. Gorman headed home to Minnesota in hopes of earning enough money to return to school. His job involved working in 110-degree heat in a cowhide factory, while wearing knee-high rubber boots, elbow-length rubber gloves and a rubber apron.

"There was a stockyard in the town where I grew up," Dr. Gorman said.

The cowhide would come into the factory in boxcars. The hides arrived pre-folded into squares and tied with twine.

"We cut the twine, unfolded them and then laid them out to be placed on hooks," Dr. Gorman said.

The hides then would go through a processing vat to remove the hair. The hides next went through another vat for tanning and dying, before the hides were placed on a table to be cut in half and finished.

"It was really hot," Dr. Gorman said. "You can imagine what it smelled like."

At the end of his shift, Dr. Gorman said his clothes were so malodorous that Metzen's wife, Leslie, told their boarder to take them off in the garage to be laundered each night. In the morning, Dr. Gorman would wear his freshly cleaned work clothes to the stock yard, before repeating the process when he returned home in the evening.

Financial Shortfall

When his financial aid information arrived in the mail toward the end of that summer, he realized his funds for sophomore year would fall $1,500 short.

"I didn't know where to get it from," Dr. Gorman said.

Without any solution, he began planning to transfer to the University of Minnesota to ease his financial burden and to continue his education. Dr. Gorman was so convinced that he could not afford to return to Notre Dame that he registered for fall classes at Minnesota. Word reached Fr. Riehle, who called Dr. Gorman in late August just one week before the start of the fall semester.

Fr. Riehle asked if the transfer was related to anything other than financial considerations. Upon hearing that finances played the sole factor in the decision, the priest sprung into action. He promised that he would intervene to bridge the financial gap if the student returned to campus for the start of school the following week.

"'We'll work that out,'" Dr. Gorman said Fr. Riehle told him. "'Don't worry about it. Get your stuff packed and get down here.'"

Upon Dr. Gorman's arrival for his sophomore year, he and Fr. Riehle met with June McCauslin, who headed Notre Dame's financial aid program at the time. She arranged to provide additional funding but it still did not close the shortfall entirely.

"What ended up happening was that Fr. Riehle called on a friend of his that he grew up with in Michigan," Dr. Gorman said.

Benevolent Benefactor

The friend, Michael Russo, had become a successful businessman and once told the priest to contact him if a student who he felt really good about ever needed financial assistance.

During the fall of his sophomore year, Dr. Gorman met his benefactor.

"Fr. Riehle came walking through the dining hall looking for me," Dr. Gorman recalled. The priest mentioned that he wanted the student to meet someone. They left the dining hall together and headed outside. Inside a limousine sat Dr. Gorman's patron. Fr. Riehle introduced them to each other.

"We just talked for a few minutes and I thanked him," Dr. Gorman said.

Dr. Gorman described Russo as a "very nice guy," who urged the student to go forward and be productive. They exchanged Christmas cards with each other from that point forward until Russo's death. Dr. Gorman still exchanges Christmas cards with his benefactor's wife, who lives in Florida.

Midnight Shift

Despite the financial help, Dr. Gorman maintained both of his campus jobs and continued to take on blue-collar work during the summer when he returned home from school to save money for college.

"I worked on the railroad a couple of summers pounding spikes," Dr. Gorman said. During another summer, Dr. Gorman manned the midnight shift as an assembly line worker in a brewery. The unglamorous jobs helped to keep Dr. Gorman motivated to return to school each fall, he added with a laugh.

By using the kind of high energy that the young, healthy and motivated can muster, Dr. Gorman also found time each summer to play amateur baseball during his college years.

"I always kept in touch with Fr. Riehle," Dr. Gorman said. "Whenever I have gone down there [to South Bend], I've gone to see him. I exchanged Christmas cards for all these years, too."

Diamond to Dentistry

Dr. Gorman also tried to play varsity baseball as a walk-on, non-scholarship student-athlete but he seldom left the bench to take the field during games.

Fr. Riehle loved sports and encouraged the students who wanted to pursue varsity or intramural athletics. While many of them, including Dr. Gorman, rarely played for the varsity teams if they earned a roster spot, Fr. Riehle conversed with them as if their aspirations were as important as Notre Dame's top athletes, Dr. Gorman recalled.

"He was always checking with me about how things were going," Dr. Gorman said.

After seldom playing as an infielder on the baseball team during his first three years, Dr. Gorman realized that he was not destined to become a Major League prospect. With professional baseball not part of his future, Dr. Gorman dropped baseball his senior year to focus on school and his goal of becoming a dentist.

Naturally, Fr. Riehle's strong personal interest in sports turned him into a confidant for many student-athletes. Fr. Riehle also typically was available to talk, since he seemed almost omnipresent as the athletic department's head chaplain and the Pangborn Hall rector.

"We hit it off right away," Dr. Gorman said.

However, Dr. Gorman never would have spent more than one year at Notre Dame without the strong and continuing support of Fr. Riehle.

Curfew Violation

"There is one incident that is part of my relationship with Fr. Riehle, too," Dr. Gorman said. "It's another instance where he helped me out."

As a junior living in a dormitory at Notre Dame, Dr. Gorman violated the university's strict parietal rules that regulated when members of the opposite sex could visit a residence hall. Late in his junior year, Dr. Gorman remembered escorting a female guest from his room through the hallway, into the lobby and out of the door after 2 a.m.

"As we were leaving the dorm, I could see out of the corner of my eye in the lobby that Fr. Riehle was sitting in there," Dr. Gorman said with a laugh. "So, I knew that he had seen me."

Friendly Fire?

Unsure what would happen next, Dr. Gorman confided to his friends about what occurred. His friends assured him that it would not become a "big deal," adding that Fr. Riehle liked him and would not take any action.

A couple of days passed before Dr. Gorman and Fr. Riehle next saw each other. As the rector of the dormitory, Fr. Riehle mentioned that he had an "obligation" to report the violation.

Upon receiving the report about the infraction, James Roemer, who served as the university's dean of students at the time, became "very upset," Dr. Gorman recalled learning from Fr. Riehle.

Dean Roemer's duties as a disciplinarian occasionally would bring him into "contentious relations" with undergraduates and he was satirized in student cartoons as a steel-helmet-donning autocrat, according to a press release the university issued after his death on August, 10, 2013. But such caricatures omitted his "ingenuous good will and cheerfully avuncular demeanor," the university's release added.

Fr. Riehle, knowing he needed to convince Dean Roemer to show compassion in assessing punishment, told the future dentist he hoped the infraction would not turn into a "serious" matter, Dr. Gorman remembered. In an attempt to intercede, Fr. Riehle arranged to meet with Dean Roemer and spoke well of the hard-working student and his character.

"I was going to be living off campus the next year," which would limit the dean's options in assessing potential sanctions, Dr. Gorman recalled.

As punishment, the dean required the student, who let his girlfriend stay in his room to avoid her needing to wait for a bus in the cold, to remain on campus during a vacation week his senior year to rake leaves as part of a grounds crew.

"The penalty could have been a lot tougher," Dr. Gorman recalled. "He [Fr. Riehle] felt really good about how that whole situation turned out."

Since Fr. Riehle previously had been the dean of students, he understood the need to make judgments about people. The priest also could use his powers of persuasion when he believed someone deserved the benefit of a doubt, as he did when Dr. Gorman attended Notre Dame and could have received severe punishment from Dean Roemer.

Deflect Dead-end Discussions

Fr. Riehle spoke his mind frankly but he also made an effort to avoid discussions that were dead-ends. He made an effort to preserve relationships with people and tried to sidestep hashing out differences of opinion that would end up gaining nothing but discord. Such situations require self-restraint. It is a valuable characteristic for anyone to develop.

"Suffice it to say that he and Fr. Hesburgh were about 180 degrees apart when it came to political views," Fr. Malloy said. "That's why it was funny when they ended up at Holy Cross House together."

The two clergymen and long-time colleagues both enjoyed smoking cigars together but they needed to find a way to do so without lighting up in the common living area with their fellow retired priests. To avoid potential arguments, Fr. Malloy said Fr. Riehle and Fr. Hesburgh did not debate their opposing political views.

"Like any other family, just focus on the common ground and stay away from the tricky things," Fr. Malloy said.

When they smoked cigars together, the two priests certainly did carry on a dialog.

"I'm sure they talked about everything else under the sun," Fr. Malloy said.

When Fr Riehle moved into Holy Cross House where the older priests lived when they needed assistance, neither he nor fellow resident Fr. Hesburgh were allowed to smoke inside the building, Fr. Malloy said.

To remedy the situation, Fr. Hesburgh obtained money to build a "minor wing" to create a "smoking room," Fr. Malloy said. Fr. Riehle, Fr. Hesburgh and other priests in residence at Holy Cross House thereafter could smoke cigars together.

Hitting the Highways for Hockey

"Where I really got to know Riehle was on the hockey trips by bus," Whitmer said. Fr. Riehle joined the hockey team, its coaches and the team trainer in traveling to "all points of the compass," Whitmer added.

The annual hockey trips included stamina-straining journeys from Notre Dame's campus in South Bend, Indiana, to Columbus, Ohio, the home of Ohio State University, as well as three universities in the scenic Upper Peninsula of Michigan.

"We traveled with 20 kids, one or two student managers, myself, the head coach and Fr. Riehle," Whitmer said. "We used to take the bus almost everywhere because it was a more relaxed environment. We didn't have to hassle with the airports with the gear and delays."

The round-trip drives involved hundreds of miles and a number of hours each way. The driving distance between Notre Dame and Ohio State was 285 miles and required nearly four hours and 30 minutes. But the greatest distance featured a bus trip to Michigan Tech near Copper Harbor in Houghton, Michigan, close to the western tip of the Upper Peninsula, spanning 509 miles and taking more than eight hours. The other road trips into the Upper Peninsula entailed the team bus venturing to Northern Michigan University in Marquette, Michigan, roughly 478 miles and nearly eight hours away; and a 400-mile trek to Sault Sainte Marie, Michigan, taking more than six hours to reach Lake Superior State University.

Once when the Notre Dame hockey team was going to Northern Michigan, the head coach and Whitmer traveled on the road and actually arrived in their hotel rooms just as a flight landed at a local airport with an entourage from the university that left South Bend at about the same time.

The time to travel by air was lengthened due to the need to take a connecting flight from South Bend to Marquette, Michigan.

Winter Wonderland

One night, Whitmer, Smith and Fr. Riehle were in the "wonderful town" of Duluth, Minnesota, where it was colder than "Hades" is hot, Whitmer said.

"We decided to go out," but the options were limited," Whitmer said. "We asked around a little bit and somebody mentioned the Club Saratoga."

The weather in Duluth that night was best suited for a polar bear. A walk of about 10 or 12 blocks was "so cold" that the trio would go just two or three blocks and then duck into the doorway of a store to gain relief from the wind that whipped though the hilly downtown area not far from the shoreline of Lake Superior.

Nearly frost-bitten, they arrive. Fr. Riehle is not wearing his priestly garb and he makes a quick request of his friends before they stepped inside.

"Hey guys, just call me 'Jim,'" Whitmer recalled Fr. Riehle saying. He simply wanted a nice evening out with his friends, without drawing attention to himself.

After hours on the road, the three amigos were ready to relax a bit.

"We sat on that bus for a long time," Whitmer said.

Chapter 7

DEVELOP A
SPIRITUAL LIFE

Before becoming the university's executive vice president in 1949, former Notre Dame President Fr. Theodore Hesburgh recalled joining Notre Dame's faculty in 1945, serving as the rector of Badin Hall and teaching theology as a greenhorn priest when he met then-student James Riehle.

"During that interval is when I knew Jim Riehle in Badin Hall," Fr. Hesburgh said. "He was a good guy and I was happy to see that he wanted to be a priest. And he's been a good one. He's always been interested in athletics and he kind of gravitated toward that particular profession."

It became a natural for Fr. Riehle to share his interest in sports with Notre Dame's players and coaches, as well as tend to their spiritual needs.

Pragmatic Priest

Former linebacker Ed "Duke" Scales said that he really didn't appreciate until years after he graduated from Notre Dame how "priestly" Fr. Riehle was in delivering insightful and Scripture-based homilies.

Now living in Vero Beach, Florida, Scales said Fr. Riehle spent parts of the winter away from frigid South Bend, Indiana, and visited with his brother, Al Riehle, in nearby Fort Pierce.

"I've always been pretty involved with our local Notre Dame club," Scales said. "We would invite him [Fr. Riehle] to our annual dinners and have him celebrate a Mass."

In addition, Scales also said that he attended many Monogram Club functions where Fr. Riehle presided at a Mass.

"The point is I became more impressed with his homilies every time I attended one of his Masses," Scales said. "He really displayed a very learned and spiritual side that I think a lot of guys might have missed. There was a lot more to him than simply the gruff old guy that liked to act tough and blow cigar smoke in your face. He was a man's priest."

As a military veteran and former athlete, Fr. Riehle attended Notre Dame when it was an all-male institution and understood its tradition.

"I think the more I knew about him, the more respect I developed for him," Scales said.

Rudy Razzing

Fr. Riehle and former athletic trainer John Whitmer both appeared together in the *Rudy* movie in the locker room scene before the only game that the lead character played in as a member of the Fighting Irish football team.

"I've never seen the movie," Whitmer said. "When that came out, I didn't answer my phone for a week. I was catching so much grief from a lot of my friends, associates and former athletes. It got to be taxing, shall we say."

Whitmer had a speaking role in the scene when Fr. Riehle recited his pre-game prayer before Rudy played in his only collegiate game.

When asked about his line, Whitmer said he could not remember and confessed that he tried to "sneak out" of appearing in the movie.

The movie crew came into the locker room at 7 a.m., changed the lights, moved the furniture and told Whitmer he needed to take off his glasses and wrist watch because they looked too modern. The scene needed to depict

1975 even though it was recreated in the early 1990s for the movie that premiered in 1993.

The scene also required two takes, said Whitmer, who recalled the director of the film wanting to shoot it from a different angle the second time. The second take also meant Fr. Riehle needed to lead the "Hail Mary" again but the seasoned priest had no problem remembering the lines of the prayer that he had learned as a boy.

Pre-Game Prayer

"He had a unique little prayer before the start of all of the games," Whitmer said.

The team would gather in a circle and kneel. Fr. Riehle would say the "Hail Mary" and a brief prayer immediately afterward.

"He did it so well that it really sunk home," Whitmer said.

The movie *Rudy* showed Fr. Riehle reciting the post-Hail Mary prayer and closing with "Notre Dame, our mother, pray for us."

Church Calms Quarterback

"Church has always been a very calming place for me anyway, whether it's through prayer when things are crazy or whether it's walking into an actual church," former Notre Dame quarterback Joe Theismann said. "I have always felt such a sense of peace when I'm there, whether I'm there in my mind or whether I'm there physically."

Those who had a chance to be influenced by Fr. Riehle are "better men today because of it," Theismann said.

"Fr. Hesburgh and Fr. Joyce basically ran the university," Theismann said. "But it seemed like, for us in the world of athletics, they had other duties."

Fr. Riehle provided spiritual leadership for those involved in sports, Theismann said.

Worldly Wisdom

Ordained at the age of 39, Fr. Riehle entered the priesthood as a second career and had the life experiences of a layman to use in counseling others, Theismann said.

"This was a worldly man who could talk to you about a lot of things because he had experienced them," Theismann said.

Fr. Riehle understood that the world is a competitive place and that winning mattered. But behaving the right way held high importance, too.

To that end, Fr. Riehle would say a prayer and always respect the opponent, but there was a little bit of "extra" emphasis when he mentioned Notre Dame, Theismann recalled.

Pinkett's Praise

The spiritual messages that Fr. Riehle gave did not seem limited to one denomination of Christianity, even though they came from a Catholic priest, said Allen Pinkett, a Baptist who held Notre Dame's rushing and scoring records when he graduated in 1986. The team had plenty of Christian players who were not Catholic, he added.

"But the Mass was something I always thought was special to the Notre Dame experience and especially on game day," Pinkett said.

The Mass was "powerful" for the players, Pinkett said.

"It's almost as if you were receiving a blessing before going out into the field of battle," Pinkett explained. "It wouldn't hurt to have a little bit of the Holy Spirit behind you when you are going to play. It's almost as if you felt like you could do something super-human while you were out there if you had God's blessings."

Pinkett recalled the players kneeling down in front of Fr. Riehle to be blessed by him when he entered the locker room after the team completed pre-game warm-ups.

"You knew it wasn't time to go play until you got your blessing," Pinkett said. "That served as something that was important."

Spiritual Spin

Fr. Riehle would spin his pre-game Mass homily into a "strong message," former football coach Bob Davie said. With the game approaching, Fr. Riehle's exact concluding words might vary but his sentiment never wavered when addressing the team.

"You better go win," Davie said the priest conveyed. His passion for Notre Dame and his dedicated presence were evident to everyone around the team, Davie said.

"All of the players respected him," Davie said.

Pastoral Patience

As Catholics, Joe Montana and Fr. Riehle shared the same religion. But Montana said he never heard the chaplain proselytize anyone. Fr. Riehle was open to discussing faith, religion, school, sports or practically anything on a college student's mind.

As far as interacting with people of different faiths, Fr. Riehle conducted himself as a man of integrity who transcended religious barriers. As a result, players whose beliefs differed from his own could talk to the chaplain without concern that he would attempt to impose his religious views on them, Montana said.

"He let you bring up the topic, and talk about what you wanted," Montana said. "He let you direct the conversation."

Montana noticed during his lengthy career in football that sometimes the last open seats on a team bus were next to guys who always were "trying to get you to do something different." Fr. Riehle simply wore the vestments of a priest, put people at ease and was receptive when someone approached him, Montana said.

"He was always there that way," Montana said. "There was never a question [about it]."

Fatherly Frankness

Fr. Riehle's concern for the players and frankness in assessing situations turned him into a valued confidant for many of the Notre Dame players.

"It wasn't like he was trying the change them," Montana said. "He still had his opinions and his thoughts about what the guys were questioning him about, but it was never that you should just be Catholic and make it easier or something along those lines. I think that's what people appreciated the most about him. First, he was a person to you and had your trust. And then, he allowed people the freedom to feel that they could talk to him about anything."

Since Fr. Riehle explained the Mass to everyone at the start of the season, it helped non-Catholic attendees appreciate the service.

"You understand what's going on, as opposed to standing there and just going through the motions," Montana said.

Spiritual Symbol

"He was the symbol, actually, of the spiritual aspect of our team," former Notre Dame kicker Bob Thomas said about Fr. Riehle.

"He always was leading us in prayer," Thomas said.

Fr. Riehle also stayed accessible to players, coaches, staffers and others. His willingness to chat, especially about sports, helped to break the ice and sometimes led to deeper conversations.

"He certainly was approachable and kind of a man's man," Thomas said. A key reason for that characterization of Fr. Riehle was his unvarnished and plainspoken demeanor.

Manly Man

Fr. Riehle viewed pressure-laden situations from a spiritual perspective as a way to serve the Lord and he tried to help others do likewise. He also urged people to appreciate the opportunities that they received and to enjoy life.

"He liked to smoke a cigar and he liked to have a drink on the side," former Notre Dame President Fr. Edward "Monk" Malloy said. "He was somebody who appreciated the hard work that went into being successful in athletics, particularly football. He knew the precariousness of the trade."

With the immense visibility of Notre Dame sports, Fr. Riehle realized as well as anyone the "high levels" of risk and reward associated with coaching and playing at the university, Fr. Malloy said.

"I think he tried to be a personal support for head coaches and others who were on the firing line," Fr. Malloy said. "He was very loyal to Notre Dame and to the people that represented Notre Dame, whether the fans felt the same way or not."

As for the student-athletes at Notre Dame, a hardnosed chaplain of the university's sports teams seemed to be a perfect fit. Fr. Riehle understood that playing or coaching sports at Notre Dame was demanding, pressure packed and required a commitment to winning. Former hockey coach Charles "Lefty" Smith, who later became the director of Notre Dame's Loftus Center between 1987 and 2011, described Fr. Riehle as a great role model for young people.

Love the Sinner

Professor Szewczyk, whose five daughters included one who only survived two weeks as an infant, was among the many people who would seek out Fr. Riehle for counsel when needed. Such an instance occurred when one of Szewczyk's daughters became pregnant out of wedlock.

"We went out to lunch," Szewczyk said of Fr. Riehle. The chaplain advised the professor to try to recognize that life was not coming to an end, to support his daughter the best way he could and to rely on his faith to persevere through the challenging situation.

"It worked out fine," Szewczyk said. The child who was born became Szewczyk's oldest grandson and ultimately graduated from Oklahoma State University with a degree in journalism. Thanks to Fr. Riehle's advice,

Szewczyk's efforts to be a loving and supportive father and grandfather in the face of difficult circumstances proved to be just what the family needed.

Reverential Respect

One characteristic that distinguished Fr. Riehle as a priest was the reverential way that he consecrated the bread and wine to become the body and blood of Christ during the Eucharistic prayer of a Catholic Mass, Gerry Faust said. Fr. Riehle extended his arms upward and held the bread, also known by Catholics as a "host," with great respect, Faust recalled. Faust added that it was easy for both Catholics and non-Catholics to recognize the priest's devotion in performing his role as the celebrant of a religious service.

In Catholic services, the host is the true presence of Christ. Fr. Riehle's dignified handling of the host served as a visual demonstration that the transformation of bread and wine in that part of the religious service by the priest truly was something extraordinary.

Part of the hockey team's spiritual ritual consisted of Fr. Riehle conducting a pre-game Mass, usually either in his hotel room or the coach's room. The experiences on the road trips helped to build bonds and let each of the players, the coaches and the trainer build a really "good relationship" with the team chaplain, Whitmer said.

When the Mass was held in the sitting room of a hotel room, Whitmer, a non-Catholic who described himself as "not-much-of-a churchgoer," usually stayed in the adjacent bedroom.

"I don't know that much about Catholicism, and the whys and what not's about it, but I respect it greatly," said Whitmer, who added that his move into the next room was his way of "showing respect" and Fr. Riehle knew it.

Even though he does not attend church regularly, Whitmer said he believes in doing the "right thing" and treating people properly.

"If you do that, you're practicing a lot of different aspects of many different beliefs," Whitmer said.

Collar-wearing Conservative

Fr. Riehle was "very conservative" and always wore his collar when sitting with the basketball team, said its former coach Richard "Digger" Phelps, who only wanted priests who donned the distinctive and visible symbol of Catholic clergy to serve as team chaplain.

"I'll never forget when I first came here [to Notre Dame] and I had a meeting with priests," Phelps said. "About four or five showed up and he was one of them. And I said, 'It has always impressed me coming from the East Coast that the fans are always looking for a priest on the bench, whether it is football or basketball. So, I want a priest on the bench, both home and away, with a collar on.' There were a lot of priests at Notre Dame who wouldn't wear collars, so they were never [team] chaplain."

Fr. Riehle served as chaplain for the basketball team from 1971 until the early 2000s when his health no longer allowed him to continue. He attended many games himself. If he was unavailable for any reason, Fr. Riehle arranged for another priest to sit courtside with the Notre Dame basketball team. Whatever priest served as the team chaplain for a particular game wore a clerical collar to reflect the university's Catholic identity.

Fast-Break Mass

The term "fast-break" usually is limited to the basketball game itself when a team quickly advances the ball down the floor to score. Fr. Riehle gave the term an additional meaning when it came to the speed of the Masses that he celebrated for the basketball team just hours before a game. A traditional Mass easily could last an hour but Fr. Riehle was able to complete one in just 18 minutes, including the sermon, super-fan Ed O'Rourke said.

Notre Dame still holds a Mass before every game for the basketball team's players and coaches. Skip Myer, the basketball team's athletic trainer, tells the priest that dinner will be served in 20 minutes. The chaplain who celebrates the Mass is expected to start and finish within that time frame.

Fr. Riehle was as dependable as a Swiss watch in fitting his Masses into that tight schedule. In basketball, a buzzer beater is a successful shot that is released before the expiration of the game clock. If Fr. Riehle received a won-loss record for keeping his pre-game Masses within the 20-minute time frame, he would have been undefeated.

Memorable Medals

The pre-game Mass, in particular, generated a feeling among football team members that was "just incredible," former football coach Lou Holtz said. The experience was enhanced when Fr. Riehle handed each player, coach and attendee of the Mass a religious medal as they exited whatever church or chapel was used for the service. Each medal distributed after a pre-game Mass would feature the image of a particular saint or another religious figure. Fr. Riehle would hand out a different medal for "each and every" game, Holtz added.

Dick Rosenthal, Notre Dame's athletic director between 1987 and 1995, saved all of the medals given out at the Masses during the 1988 national championship football season and had them gold-plated.

"He gave them to us as a gift of the championship season," said Holtz, who added he still treasures the religious medals that Fr. Riehle handed him.

The bestowing of religious medals prior to each game became a tradition. The recipients felt as though they were part of a "very religious institution" that was extraordinarily special, Holtz said.

"I think it's the love and the feeling for Notre Dame and the spirituality of Notre Dame," Holtz said. "It's about academics and it's about sports but it's also about spirituality. I think Fr. Riehle did a great job in bringing the spirituality of Notre Dame to our football team and to the student body in general."

Pangborn Express

Fr. Riehle's 5 p.m. Mass on Sunday when he served as rector of Pangborn Hall became known as the "Pangborn Express." The nickname that students gave the Mass probably stemmed from its brevity. From start to finish, the Mass lasted less than 25 minutes, including the homily, Holtz said.

"I went there one time and I want to tell you it was jammed with students," Holtz said. "He interacted with all the players and the students at Pangborn on a daily basis."

Fr. Riehle had a "very positive spiritual impact on a lot of the players," Holtz said.

Fr. Riehle became well known around campus even among non-athletes for his short Masses and homilies, omitting any music, Fr. Malloy said.

"He would not be described as anybody who was big into high liturgy or anything like that," said Fr. Malloy, who added that Fr. Riehle always kept his homilies "to the point."

Fr. Malloy never attended Fr. Riehle's Pangborn Express Mass but confirmed that the abbreviated religious service was popular among students at Notre Dame.

"I just knew about it [the Pangborn Express] by reputation," Fr. Malloy said.

With demanding academic requirements at Notre Dame, "your time is precious," Whitmer said. As a result, Fr. Riehle's Pangborn Express Mass each Sunday catered to busy students.

Spiritual Service

When Fr. Riehle took a trip to California to play golf, he asked O'Rourke, the friend accompanying him on the journey, if he wanted to assist him as an altar server. Fr. Riehle offered to celebrate the Mass in Latin. But O'Rouke's recollection of the prayers to recite during the traditional Latin Mass had faded since the Second Vatican Council decided in the 1960s to allow Catholics worldwide to celebrate in their native languages.

O'Rourke recited a line that he remembered from the Latin services that caused Fr. Riehle to stop suddenly. The priest then said, "That's my line."

Fr. Riehle was known for his sense of humor, but that instance marked one occasion when his friend injected a bit of levity into the service unintentionally. Unfazed, Fr. Riehle completed the rest of the Mass in Latin and O'Rourke avoided any further mistakes.

Selection Sunday

Many years before the NCAA Basketball Tournament became "March Madness," featuring a nationally televised CBS program announcing the qualifying teams on "Selection Sunday," Fr. Riehle had developed his own form of anointing chosen ones as readers for Sunday Masses. Fr. Riehle's version of "Selection Sunday" typically took place in the living rooms of the homes he might visit to celebrate a Mass with family, friends and their neighbors.

The pretend Masses that he led as a child proved to be a great training ground. Much as he did as the oldest child in his family, Fr. Riehle directed the proceedings of the Masses that he led as an adult.

"Mass at home was a big part of the Riehle family life," said Jeannine Ruse, his niece through her marriage to Fr. Riehle's nephew Jim Ruse. "Uncle Jim said many a holiday Mass."

Part of that tradition included Fr. Riehle's selection of readers for the service from those in attendance.

"Whether you volunteered or not was irrelevant to Uncle Jim," Jeannine Ruse said.

Prayer List

At times, Fr. Riehle's tough-guy exterior may have made him seem a bit chauvinistic as if he was a throwback to the days when Notre Dame was an all-male institution, his Monogram Club friend Marty Allen said.

But unknown to most people is that Fr. Riehle actually had a "tremendous devotion" to expectant mothers and children, Allen said. The chaplain developed a lengthy prayer list that he included in the Mass kit he took with him various places. Many names on the list featured expectant mothers and children who Fr. Riehle had been asked to include in his prayers, regardless of their faith, Allen added.

Fr. Riehle included Allen's own daughter on the priest's prayer list, along with that of a non-Catholic friend of Allen's whose grandchild was suffering from spina bifida, a congenital abnormality in which part of the spinal cord protrudes through the spinal column and leaves a person highly vulnerable to neurological impairment.

"He was very sincere about his prayer list," Allen said. "It was just kind of interesting, the irony that he might have seemed chauvinistic but that in reality his greatest love and concern was for expectant mothers and children."

Prayer Partner

When James Brady and his wife Nan, Fr. Riehle's niece, lived in Greensburg, Pennsylvania, one of their hangouts was a restaurant/bar in nearby South Greensburg. Fr. Riehle sometimes joined his relatives there when he visited.

"One evening, one of our friends, Terry McCormick, approached me to ask a favor," Brady said. "It seems his nephew, a high school senior and a talented football player recruited by a number of Division One schools, had been in an accident, was paralyzed and would never play football again. He would be in the hospital for some time and Terry was naturally concerned. He inquired if I would ask Fr. Riehle to call the boy and talk with him to cheer him up. I said I would speak with Jim. I did and Jim did call the boy. I expected Jim to have a short conversation and be done with it. Terry told me later, Jim did call and talked with the boy for some 45 minutes. The call did wonders for the boy."

About a year later, Fr. Riehle and Brady were talking. Suddenly, Fr. Riehle asked how "so and so" was doing, Brady said.

"I asked who he was talking about," Brady said. "He named the young man. I had to tell Jim I had forgotten. Jim told me he prayed for him every day. Kind of says it all."

On the exterior, Fr. Riehle could be as stern as anyone but he also could empathize with those who struggled, lift their spirits and seek to alleviate their burdens through the power of prayer.

Remarkable Recovery

Notre Dame priests, including Fr. Riehle, concelebrated a Mass at the Basilica of the Sacred Heart in the aftermath of a 1992 bus accident involving the women's swim team that left two freshmen dead and another paralyzed.

The basilica was so full of concelebrants and worshippers that many people needed to stand outside.

The paralyzed swimmer, Haley Scott (DeMaria), moved a toe one week later and ultimately regained her mobility after a number of surgeries and many months of rehabilitation.

"I visited Haley in the hospital several times as did many others, including I am confident Fr. Riehle, but we were never there together," said Fr. Malloy, who was president of the university at the time of the bus crash.

"She herself is confident that the great outpouring of prayers was what got her through," Fr. Malloy said. "She eventually became a Catholic and attributed that choice to the way that the Notre Dame family supported her all through her ordeal."

DeMaria, now married and the mother of two boys, later resumed athletic competition at Notre Dame and became Monogram Club president in 2013. She also has been able to play in the club's annual Riehle Open golf tournament, despite lingering effects from her injuries.

Personal Invitation

Joe Tybor, who covered Notre Dame football and basketball for the *Chicago Tribune* between 1989 and 1996, recalled one time when Fr. Riehle invited him to attend Mass with the football team. The Mass took place on Aug. 15 during the Feast of the Assumption, a holy day of obligation that requires Catholics to attend church on a day other than the Sabbath. The Mass, commemorating the assumption of the body of Jesus' mother Mary into heaven, took place when the football team was practicing twice a day, leaving little time for the reporter to cover the action of the day, write his stories and still find time to attend church. The Mass was held in the basement chapel of the Basilica of the Sacred Heart on Notre Dame's campus.

"I felt quite honored to have been invited to that [Mass] because I know that most outsiders are not invited," said Tybor, who now handles press relations for the Illinois Supreme Court. "He was always very kind to me. He attended almost every practice."

Fr. Riehle always offered a cheery "hello" to the journalist and developed a good relationship with him, as the team chaplain routinely did with people, Tybor said.

"I loved the man," said Tybor, who described Fr. Riehle as "busy" but still "very helpful."

Before receiving an offer from the *Chicago Tribune* to switch beats and cover the Notre Dame football and basketball teams, Tybor, a law school graduate, covered legal affairs for the newspaper. Upon agreeing to change assignments, Tybor told his managing editor that he had been able to cover one institution, the Judiciary, and liked the prospect of writing about another institution, Notre Dame football.

In 1993, while still working at the *Chicago Tribune*, Tybor started his own website, IrishEyes.com. That website, now known as notredame.scout.com, still follows Notre Dame football and actually appeared on the Internet before ESPN, Tybor said.

Occasional 'Ghost' Sightings

The team chaplain's connection with athletes often extended beyond the playing field, continued past their graduations and stretched throughout their lives.

Fr. Riehle was one of two Notre Dame priests who concelebrated the 1974 wedding Mass of former All-American football player David Casper and his wife, Susan (Andersen) Casper, in the Basilica of the Sacred Heart on the university's campus.

Casper, nicknamed "The Ghost" by his teammates, later became a star in the NFL, where he was named a Pro Bowl tight end five times. In addition, his pass catching and blocking helped the Oakland Raiders beat the Minnesota Vikings 32-14 in Super Bowl XI on January 9, 1977.

The next season during the 1977 playoffs, Casper grabbed a 10-yard touchdown pass to win a double-overtime game for the Raiders against the then-Baltimore Colts. The winning catch would not have been possible without his 42-yard reception on a post pattern that allowed the Raiders to tie the game with a field goal before the end of regulation late in the fourth quarter. The memorable catch became known in pro football lore as "Ghost to the Post."

In 1978, Casper scored an unprecedented game-winning touchdown in a regular season matchup against the San Diego Chargers, an American Football Conference rival. With just 10 seconds left in the contest and the Chargers leading by six points, Ken "The Snake" Stabler, the Raiders' quarterback, was on the verge of getting tackled to end the game. But he intentionally fumbled the football forward in a last-ditch try to keep the play alive. The ball advanced 13 yards to San Diego's 11-yard-line, where Oakland running back Pete Banaszek batted it closer to the goal line. Casper spotted the ball and deflected it with his foot at the five-yard-line into the end zone, where he fell on it to give his team an improbable victory.

Holy Roller

The famous play became known as "The Holy Roller." In response, the NFL later added a provision, commonly known as the "Dave Casper rule," to allow only a player who fumbles the ball to advance it after a referee gives the "two-minute" warning before halftime and the end of regulation. As a result, that play forever will remain one of a kind in the NFL.

Casper, traded by the Raiders midway through the 1980 season to the Houston Oilers for the high price of a first-round draft pick and two second-round draft picks, was inducted into the Pro Football Hall of Fame in 2002 after playing for 11 years in the NFL between 1974 and 1984.

One might think that an acclaimed Super Bowl winner and the only player from Notre Dame's 1973 national championship team elected to the Pro Football Hall of Fame would receive fawning adulation whenever he visited his alma mater after his graduation. If Casper received such treatment, it did not come from Fr. Riehle. To the contrary, the chaplain remained true to his curmudgeonly form whenever he spotted "The Ghost" at a reunion.

'Ghost' Buster

Until the chaplain's last days, he admonished Casper for not "taking care" of the religious medals that the priest gave to each of the players at pre-game Masses, the Pro Football Hall of Fame inductee recalled. The ribbing showed that Fr. Riehle adhered to no statute of limitations in telling former players who he led spiritually during their college days exactly what was on his mind, no matter how accomplished they became.

It seemed Fr. Riehle wanted to remind the football hero that one's spiritual life should take precedence above worldly success.

"He was very, very persistent," Casper said.

As a three-year starter for Notre Dame's football team, Casper was voted the Most Valuable Player (MVP) and became an Academic All-American. He graduated cum laude with a degree in economics, gained acceptance to the Omicron Delta Epsilon Honor Society for Economics and received a postgraduate scholarship from the NCAA. Casper, now a financial advisor with Northwestern Mutual Financial Network, was chosen as the tight end for the *Sports Illustrated* All-Time Dream Team and the All-Century Team.

Regardless of any worldly accomplishments that people may achieve, Fr. Riehle tried to offer them spiritual leadership when such opportunities arose.

Methodist Medal Collector

One former Notre Dame football player who valued the religious medals that Fr. Riehle gave him was David "Kris" Haines. The wide receiver confirmed that he kept at least 20 of them.

"My favorite was St. Christopher," said Haines, who added that he used to wear that medal. He also enjoyed the medal of St. Jude, the patron saint of desperate causes.

The medals that Haines had not given away included ones for St. Francis of Assisi, St. Joseph, St. Vincent, St. Martin, the Virgin Mary, St. Michael and St. Guadalupe.

Haines, a Methodist, ironically retained his religious medals but lost track of most of his other collectibles from playing football for Notre Dame.

"I don't have my jerseys, game balls, letter jackets, monogram blanket or blue blazer," Haines said.

Haines donated a ring given to him for playing in a bowl game to support a charity championed by Steve Beuerlein, a former Notre Dame and NFL quarterback. Beuerlein not only raised money to aid in the fight against amyotrophic lateral sclerosis (ALS), commonly known as Lou Gehrig's disease, but gained increased federal funding after testifying before a U.S. Senate subcommittee in May 2000 by sharing the story of his high school teammate, Jeff Sherer, developing the disease. Beuerlein's friend, a once-powerful offensive lineman, died in February 2003 but the battle against ALS continues.

'Green Jersey' Game Homily

Rarely is the sermon of a clergyman long remembered but Haines recalled one Fr. Riehle homily more than 25 years later. The homily took place on October 22, 1977, during a Mass before what became known as the "green jersey game."

Head Coach Dan Devine devised a way to fire up his team by changing the color of the jerseys from navy blue and white to kelly green and gold before a key home game against the University of Southern California. The motivational move sparked a 49-19 victory for Notre Dame against the rival Trojans. The Fighting Irish continued to wear green for the rest of Devine's tenure at the school. At that pre-game Mass, Haines recalled Fr. Riehle telling the team not to expect divine intervention on the playing field.

"I think God's got something better to do today than referee the Notre Dame-USC game," Haines recalled Fr. Riehle saying. There are people on the other team, Haines said the priest added.

The Notre Dame team then entered the stadium with their green jerseys to the enthusiastic support of the home crowd on their way to winning the 1977 national championship.

"He was always inspirational," Haines said about Fr. Riehle.

That particular pre-game Mass featured elderly ladies who were kneeling in the front row, Haines said. The Mass usually was held just for the team but Fr. Riehle occasionally would learn about particular people who wanted to attend as a special celebration and he would invite them as his guests. In this case, the ladies received the additional honor of sitting in front.

Humble in Hamburg

Haines reminisced about that Mass with Fr. Riehle more than 20 years later when both of them participated in a charity event with a Notre Dame alumni team before 18,500 spectators at Volkspark Stadium in Hamburg, Germany, on July 8, 2000.

Fr. Riehle passed out his traditional religious medals after his pre-game Mass. After Fr. Riehle celebrated the team Mass before the charity game in Germany, Haines said he approached the chaplain to convey the significance of the priest's homily before the "green jersey game" against USC in 1978.

"You made a big impact before the USC game," Haines said he told Fr. Riehle. "He looked at me and said, 'Kris, I never thought you listened to me.'"

The response was typical of Fr. Riehle's quick quips that amused players before games, Haines said.

The German tabloid newspaper *Hamburger Morgan Post* may have been prescient when it mentioned the Friday before the charity game that Notre Dame team chaplain Rev. James Riehle, C.S.C., was the Fighting Irish representative with the best connections "to the top."

With Fr. Riehle once again on the sidelines during a close game in the waning seconds, Notre Dame's alumni team defeated the Hamburg Blue Devils, 14-10. Proceeds from the game benefitted Kinder Helfen Kindern (Kids Helping Kids), as well as a charity designated by the Notre Dame alumni players.

Greg Mattison, alumni head coach and then-Fighting Irish defensive coordinator, said during the last time out before the game's final play—with Hamburg just eight yards away from scoring the game-winning touchdown—that legend and reality tell us that Notre Dame players always can dig deep when needed. On the game's final play, Notre Dame's Ivory Covington intercepted a pass thrown to the corner of the end zone to clinch the win.

Spiritual Rise of 'Rocket'

Raghib "Rocket" Ismail, a wide receiver from Wilkes-Barre, Pennsylvania, may have been among the best kickoff return men in the history of college football. He stood next to Fr. Riehle one day while they watched an intramural volleyball game. Ismail turned to Fr. Riehle and said that he was really looking forward to the upcoming football season. When Fr. Jim asked why, Ismail said it was because he enjoyed attending the pre-game Masses so much. Ironically, Ismail was introduced to the Muslim faith as a boy. Just two years after his football-playing days at Notre Dame concluded and he had left for professional football, Ismail became a committed Christian. He now discusses his conversion openly during occasional public speaking engagements.

Ismail's gridiron honors included finishing second to Brigham Young Quarterback Ty Detmer in the Heisman Trophy voting during his third and final year as a college football player before taking his blazing speed to the professional ranks. The one-time Notre Dame star talked candidly about the temptations of celebrity life that ensnared him before his wholehearted conversion to Christianity. He acknowledged enduring rocky times of personal turmoil before he consistently began to put his faith into action. Ismail credited Fr. Riehle for serving as a source of spiritual strength.

Ismail said he believed his conversion grew from prayers offered for him by a combination of people, including his grandmother, parishioners from his hometown church in Wilkes-Barre and many others.

"I was a beneficiary of the prayers going up," Ismail said. In Ismail's view, the grace of God manifested itself perfectly on his behalf. Ismail described the blessing he felt as a "grace" because he said he didn't really do anything to deserve it.

Meaningful Masses

Fr. Riehle's messages during Mass wielded a positive influence, Ismail said.

"He was so matter of fact in expressing the love of God," Ismail said. Fr. Riehle would recall times when Christ or one of his disciples would face seemingly insurmountable obstacles. Rather than succumb to the difficulties, people would come close to a breaking point, plaintively "cry out to the Lord," and then claim that God lightened the weight of their earthly obligations, he explained.

Despite his prominence as a football star, Ismail said that he could identify with the people that Fr. Riehle cited from the bible who faced daunting challenges. As the Notre Dame football team began to win consistently, the media spotlight and fan expectations intensified. Ismail said he felt "unprepared" for the attention and the adulation that was thrust upon him. From a modest background, he became a touchdown-scoring sensation. His reputation grew quickly as followers of college football watched his on-the-field exploits on Saturday afternoons each fall.

"Looking back on it, I didn't know that it was going to be that big, as far as the attention that Notre Dame gets," Ismail said. "Especially since we were winning, it was even more amplified. I really wasn't equipped to be able to handle a lot of the pressures that went with it and a lot of the expectations. It used to overwhelm me at times."

Special Sanctuary

The game day Masses, blessings and prayers offered by Fr. Riehle became a refuge from the distractions and pressures of the world, Ismail said.

"It always felt like, because of that blessing that he would give us, I'm okay," Ismail said.

That sense of reassurance was important, since the temptations of the world can pull sports heroes in directions other than those that may please God, Ismail said.

"I really wasn't giving everything that I had to God," Ismail said. "I was being drawn very subtly but very seductively by the trappings of the world, and the quote-unquote 'American Dream,'" Ismail said.

Without recognizing the source of strength it provided during his college years at Notre Dame, Ismail said Fr. Riehle's spiritual presence as the team chaplain served as a tether in the midst of life's storms that otherwise could have swept him away.

"Even though I didn't know at the time that it was an anchor for me, looking back on it, I can really see how strategically the Lord placed it in my life to keep me from drifting too far," Ismail said.

The media swarm that was focused on the Notre Dame team seemed pervasive and sometimes all-consuming but the Masses offered a temporary sanctuary from the relentless demands of the world, Ismail said.

"I always felt kind of safe when we would go to the Masses and be in that environment," Ismail said. "It had a lot to do with the dynamics of what was happening inside of me at that time."

Record-Setting Remuneration

Ismail acknowledged an appreciation for supportive people and for the memories they retain about their interactions with him. His profile as a football icon heightened in 1991 when he signed the highest-paying contract that ever had been given to a football player up to then. He inked a four-year "personal services" contract with Bruce McNall, owner of the Toronto Argonauts of the Canadian Football League (CFL), for a guaranteed $14 million. The team gained additional attention because two of its co-owners were hockey legend Wayne Gretsky and comedic actor John Candy. During his inaugural season with Toronto in 1991, Ismail was a CFL All-Star and the Most Valuable Player in the league's Grey Cup championship game. The latter honor followed an 87-yard kickoff return that propelled his team to the title game win against the Winnipeg Blue Bombers.

The next year was a disappointing one professionally for Ismail, as well as for the owners of the Toronto Argonauts. They suffered together with a losing record and reduced attendance at the team's home games. Toronto did not re-sign its championship quarterback from the Grey Cup-winning season and the team struggled. The Argonauts also publicly announced before that season that Ismail would be given the ball on 40-50 percent of the team's offensive plays. That unconventional focus on one player rather than the team drew the ire of fellow All-Star's on the squad and morale sagged.

Toronto's poor start to the season triggered the firing of the head coach who led the Argonauts to the league title the previous year. The Argonauts' record slipped to 6-12 and it seemed to be in everyone's best interest for Ismail to leave for the NFL, where Ismail could display his skills in front of an American audience that seldom had a chance to watch CFL games. Another plus was that it would allow Ismail to move forward when it became clear his previous contract with the Argonauts would not be fulfilled by the team's troubled owner.

Unraveling Universe

"The guy who was paying me was in jail," Ismail said. By the time Ismail and his advisers learned that McNall's financial empire was crumbling, the football star ended up well down a list of the owner's creditors with no realistic chance of recouping any of the money that was owed to him.

The spiritual foundation that Ismail had built with the help of Fr. Riehle and others aided in the transition. But the journey proved to be emotionally heart-wrenching for the celebrated athlete.

Before the next football season in 1994, Ismail, 24 years old at the time, reflected on the tumultuous time in his life and returned to South Bend to resume working on the completion of his degree at Notre Dame. He recalled having just finalized a $3 million contract to play football for the Los Angeles Raiders during the next two seasons. Although sports celebrities often are idolized by devoted fans, neither the acclaim nor the money brought joy to Ismail. At that time of soul-searching, it was an inexpensive gift that led to an epiphany for Ismail.

"My sister sent me a book," Ismail said. While reading it, Ismail remembered feeling the ill effects of "sin and transgression" for the way he was living at that time. He recalled sitting in the kitchen of an off-campus apartment he was renting in South Bend that summer. He began to read the book while taking a break from writing a paper on his laptop computer for a media class. As he read the book, Ismail said he felt a connection with a powerful testimonial of conversion shared by a woman who overcame personal tribulations through a deepened faith in God.

Respectful Repentance

"I just felt the prompting to repent," said Ismail, who spontaneously prayed to God for his life not to be held captive by the alluring siren songs of the world.

"I literally got on my knees right there at the table," Ismail said. "I repented and I asked Him to forgive me. Then the weirdest thing happened."

Mysteriously, Ismail said he felt compelled at that moment to make a life-changing decision to abandon his will to God in the same humble way that he had seen other people do when he witnessed their personal testimonies during church services. Ismail specifically recalled attending Protestant churches and hearing people speak dramatically about experiences that led them to accept the Lord into their lives.

"There sometimes would be a common theme in a lot of the people's testimonies," Ismail said. "The theme would be that I felt burdened. I cried out to God and then there was a weight lifted off of me. And I remembered that, as I got older, I would get more sarcastic and say, 'Isn't it amazing how people have this weight lifted off of them and then people rejoice and clap and feel good about themselves.'"

However, the responsibility Ismail felt as a football hero and as the CFL's marquee player eased one day when he prayed in his apartment's kitchen.

When he concluded praying and said "amen," Ismail gained a sense of relief. He suddenly felt as though he could breathe more easily.

"I felt like a physical weight had just lifted and I was stunned," Ismail said.

Rich in Blessings

Many people might say Ismail became a rich man when he signed a record contract to play football for the Toronto Argonauts. But Ismail said he may have been most blessed on the day he prayed alone in his apartment and gained a sense of peace.

"Now, I'm a living witness," Ismail said. After praying for divine guidance in his apartment, Ismail said he embarked on a faithful journey to live each day thereafter as a Christian.

"I feel blessed to be able to say that I have definitely experienced more of the grace of God and more of His mercy in my endeavor to walk closely with him," Ismail said. A profound transformation for Ismail came when his actions reflected his values. He previously talked about living faithfully as a Christian but failed to do so 100 percent.

Ismail now attends a small, non-denominational church in Dallas with his wife and children. He has become familiar with Scripture. He cited words from the bible that describe a person's body as a temple of the "Holy Spirit of God." It may seem unusual for a sports celebrity to talk openly about religion but Ismail spoke with conviction.

Spiritual Stability

As a young man trying to navigate his way through a tumultuous time in his high-profile life, Ismail said that Fr. Riehle was a steady source of spiritual stability. Fr. Riehle's positive influence reminded Ismail of a parable about a man whose house is built on a rock, in contrast to another man whose house is on sinking sand. When battered by wind and rain, the house erected on rock survived all of nature's storms, while the house on sinking sand was destroyed.

"Fr. Jim was the man who had built on the rock," Ismail said. "I might be the guy next to him who was kind of in that sandy area. As the winds would blow, I would reach out and grab his hand and hold on until it settled down and I would see that everything was okay. And then I would run back to the sand again but it was just enough to keep me from being overwhelmed, consumed and destroyed by my own will."

From Ismail's perspective, Fr. Riehle "definitely represented the light" that Christ referred to when calling for people to become the light and salt of the Earth. At times when Ismail said he was "wandering around" in spiritual darkness, Fr. Riehle lit a spiritual path by preaching about Christ's teachings.

"One thing I like to tell people is that when you read the Synoptic Gospels, there will be accounts that are similar but one account will have a little extra information that maybe two others didn't have," Ismail said. "I used to always think, 'How come these two gospels have the same story as the third gospel but the exact specifics of it will be just a little different.'"

Ismail has learned to appreciate the different recollections of people and the details they can recall. It happens when he meets with his former Notre Dame teammates to discuss the events of the past.

"I'd have a perspective, then two other guys would have perspectives, and then one other guy would say, 'But, yeah, remember this aspect of it?'" Ismail said.

Skating Seminarians

Fr. Riehle's connection with athletes spanned the highest-paid professionals such as Ismail to amateurs who played for enjoyment and exercise. Not only had Fr. Riehle served as captain of his hockey team at St. Andrew's High School in Saginaw, Michigan, he played pickup games outdoors during the year he spent at the Sacred Heart Novitiate in Jordan, Minnesota. Fr. Riehle worked with Brother Clarence Breitenbach to build an outdoor hockey rink for use by the novitiates who were entering religious life. The pair skated on the rink and gladly recruited other postulants, who also were seeking acceptance into the Holy Cross religious order. They played quite a bit of hockey and made their own sticks.

"They had a great time skating and enjoying themselves," Smith said.

Brother Clarence supervised the prospective priests and assigned them work duties. The novitiate used a coal-burning furnace that the men needed to keep stoked. Boilers also required monitoring.

"In the meantime, we decided to make an ice rink because it was cold in that area," Brother Clarence said. They leveled out the ground near a well that provided water used to form solid ice that became their skating area each winter. The ice rink was big enough to allow two games to be played at the same time, while an adjacent area was available for free skating.

The hockey-playing season at the novitiate's manmade ice rink began in December and continued until March each year. The men played hockey routinely during their recreation period. Although Fr. Riehle spent just a single year at the novitiate on his path to the priesthood, Brother Clarence served 15 years there supervising the work and recreational activities of the prospective clergymen.

Ingenuity on the Ice

Brother Clarence and the postulants showed ingenuity by converting a donated truck that had a 1,000-gallon tank into an ice-resurfacing machine. The truck was placed on a trailer and a bung was put underneath the vehicle to fill a large hole in the tank where water otherwise would empty. To spread the water evenly along the ice during resurfacing, the men drilled small holes in an eight-foot pipe that they attached across the width of the vehicle.

"Then we'd hook up the tractor and we'd use that to go around," Brother Clarence said. "We could make that [ice] look like a table top; it was really nice."

To avoid the expense of buying hockey sticks, the postulants used an encyclopedia to learn how to make their own. They produced 100 hockey sticks at a time by adopting mass production techniques.

"They weren't that great, but they served the purpose," Brother Clarence said.

When the novitiate closed in 1967, Brother Clarence moved to Notre Dame and teamed up with Fr. Riehle the following year to become founding members of a lunchtime hockey group. The Notre Dame staffers who played hockey skated at noon and had use of a new campus ice rink for themselves.

"That was really fun," Brother Clarence said.

Surprising Confession

When asked if he could recall any examples of Fr. Riehle's hard-nosed play at the novitiate, Brother Clarence gave a surprising confession.

"I had an advantage over the guys who were there. I was a professed religious and they were novices. So, they kind of laid off [me], but I did a little checking. I could play a little rougher than they could," Brother Clarence said with a chuckle.

The location of the makeshift ice rink nearby railroad tracks gave Brother Clarence an idea to position railroad ties along the perimeter of the ice. Three railroad ties stacked on top of each other three-and-a-half feet high created boards that surrounded the playing area.

"We got all of the novices out there and they changed the ties every once in a while," Brother Clarence said.

"We could bounce the puck off of the ties but you couldn't lift it that high," Brother Clarence said. "It was a rough-and-tumble game. When we first got started, one guy went out there, took a swipe of the puck and hit a guy in the mouth. And he spit out a tooth right off the bat."

Digging His Buddies' Graves

When Brother Clarence came to Notre Dame, one of his chief duties became digging graves.

The burial plots he prepared at the Holy Cross community seminary ultimately would be used by his friends in the religious community. Brother Clarence literally worked hard to put his buddies six feet under.

While Brother Clarence displayed his unconventional devotion by preparing the final resting places of his fellow Congregation of Holy Cross (C.S.C.) community members, Fr. Riehle served Notre Dame students and athletes who typically had decades of life ahead of them.

Nun for a Niece

One of Fr. Riehle's nieces, Mary Jean Brucksch, attended the first Mass he celebrated as a priest when she was in elementary school and later became a 17-year-old Discalced Carmelite Nun, Sr. Mary Angela. Her unusual looking last name is pronounced "Brooks." She took the name Mary Angela when she became a nun at a cloistered monastery just outside Grand Rapids, Michigan, where she now is the "mother superior" to the members of her religious community.

When Fr. Riehle was a baby, Sr. Mary Angela's mother, Lorena, used to push him around in his stroller. Lorena later wrote a 1986 poetry book titled, "Deep Steeples."

"They were kind of close because when my mother had her first child, she named him Jim," Sr. Mary Angela said. In fact, Sr. Mary Angela's brother followed in his Uncle Jim's path and became a priest, Fr. James L. Brucksch, who Pope Benedict gave the title of "monsignor" on December 23, 2011. Msgr. Brucksch is in Michigan's Diocese of Gaylord.

A Family First

Sr. Mary Angela remembered her Uncle Jim as personable and likable.

"He liked everybody, too," Sr. Mary Angela said. "That's probably the secret. He loved a lot, and so everybody loved him."

Fr. Riehle visited his sister Lorena and her family in Saginaw when Sr. Mary Angela was a girl.

After she became a nun, Sr. Mary Angela stayed in touch with her uncle and invited him to visit the convent to say Mass several times. He loved doing so. In fact, the nuns at the convent were some of the cheeriest people he had ever met, Fr. Riehle wrote in a letter to his niece.

"'You're happy, busy people,'" Sr. Mary Angela recalled her uncle writing to her. "'I've never met a happier group.' It was quite a compliment coming from him."

His perception was accurate, his niece confirmed.

"We are a very happy group," said Sr. Mary Angela, who added her Uncle Jim seemed "really impressed" with the spirit of the nuns each time he visited his niece at the convent.

Contemplative at the Convent

Normally talkative, Fr. Riehle seemed on the "quiet side" when visiting the convent, as if he was a little in awe, Sr. Mary Angela said. When Fr. Riehle no longer could drive, one of the athletic coaches from Notre Dame chauffeured him to the convent to visit his niece. Not surprisingly, the sports-loving chaplain either was returning from or heading to a football game, she recalled.

"He always assured me of his prayers and I always assured him of mine," Sr. Mary Angela said.

Sr. Mary Angela saved the handwritten copies of her uncle's homilies when he celebrated Masses at her monastery. He devoted his first sermon there on June 29, 1986, to seeking God's mercy, despite our own imperfections.

"We are all sinners," Fr. Riehle told the nuns. "If we say we have no sin, the truth is not in us. God needs sinners. God uses human means for His greatest works. We are not angels or saints—yet. God needs sinners because of his mercy. God loves us. He doesn't hate us; He loves us. He loves us because we are His creatures. He needs sinners so that His mercy can come down and transform that soul by a veritable 'Miracle' of His grace—not by our own perfection—into a soul who will help the church, who will really do something for the good of the church and other souls."

During his second visit to the monastery on June 14, 1987, Fr. Riehle told the nuns he ended up in the hospital after his previous visit due to a "rare blood infection." With his characteristic wit, Fr. Riehle said he became so close to holiness during his last stay that his "system couldn't stand it."

"He was very affirming in his manner," Sr. Mary Angela said. "He made sure you were on the right road."

Fr. Riehle also could converse in a way to help someone "feel good," Sr. Mary Angela said.

"He was just fatherly and easy to talk to," Sr. Mary Angela said.

Creative Collector

To help the nuns, Fr. Riehle saved stamps from unsolicited letters that contained an envelope inside with unused postage. He found an alternative use for the stamps by giving them to his niece. He had asked if the nuns in her order could use the stamps because he otherwise would just throw them away. The nuns soaked off the stamps to use as postage when they needed to mail any letters. Her Uncle Jim saved the stamps year-round and sent them to his niece annually around Easter.

"I only counted them once, because I wanted some idea of how much money he was saving us: $300-plus," Sr. Mary Angela said. "That's a lot of stamps."

Binoculars for Bird Watching

The generosity showed Fr. Riehle's sense of thrift. He also donated several pairs of binoculars to the nuns for bird-watching.

"They were real heavy and you could tell they were quite old," said Sr. Mary Angela, who speculated they may have been the first pairs he owned. The nuns still use the binoculars.

"One of them was really ancient," Sr. Mary Angela recalled with a laugh. The leather case for that pair kept falling apart as if it was "disintegrating," but the binoculars still worked, she added.

For someone who only visited the convent on rare occasions, Fr. Riehle conveyed a humble paternalistic presence and strong spirituality that outlasted his own life.

Chapter 8

LIVE TO LEAVE
A LEGACY

The University of Notre Dame's storied football tradition features its legendary 1924 backfield known as the "Four Horsemen," seven Heisman Trophy winners and a passionate national fan base. The school's football history includes the motivating speeches of famed football coach Knute Rockne, the stoic strength of dying halfback George Gip and the end-of-the-game kicking heroics of daily churchgoer Harry Oliver. However, its iconic name conveys more than just a litany of athletic achievements.

Students, alumni, faculty and fans often describe the university, named "Notre Dame" to honor the mother of God, as a special place for reasons of faith. As a university founded in November 26, 1842, by Rev. Edward Sorin, a 28-year-old French priest with the Congregation of the Holy Cross, Notre Dame's religious roots are immediately evident upon glancing at "Touchdown Jesus," a colorful, multi-story mosaic of Christ. That unique artwork decorates the façade of the campus library and faces the football stadium.

Despite the distinctive architecture, Notre Dame may be best known for the personal stories of those who inspired others. On that measure, Notre Dame shines among American universities. Fr. Riehle, who served Notre Dame for decades in many key roles spanning the turbulent student rebellion era of the 1960s and the dawn of a new millennium in the early 2000s, accepted his responsibilities with the obedience that is expected of a priest.

Fr. Riehle is remembered by those who knew him for serving the university faithfully before he died at the age of 83 on October 29, 2008. While others held higher-ranking positions and received more kudos than Fr. Riehle, he connected with the famous and those often overlooked.

Vitale's View

Dick Vitale, the irrepressible ESPN basketball commentator, said he enjoyed exchanging pleasantries with Fr. Riehle at Notre Dame sporting events. Vitale's daughters Sherri and Terri attended Notre Dame on tennis scholarships, so he and his family would gather together during those years for home football game weekends when Fr. Riehle would take part in supporting the team.

"If he'd see me at a football weekend, he'd say 'Dickie V., we're in great shape. I feel it. I spoke to the big guy,'" Vitale recalled.

Vitale said he enjoyed sharing friendly banter with Fr. Riehle during the home football weekends, particularly at Notre Dame pep rallies.

"I'd joke around and fool around," Vitale said.

Fr. Riehle exhibited genuine zeal for the Fighting Irish. Vitale said he vividly remembers Fr. Riehle approaching him and giving a "thumbs up" signal about the upcoming game.

"Man, we're in great shape today," Vitale recalled Fr. Riehle saying. "I can just feel it. The prayers are being answered for a big W here in South Bend."

Quarterback Tom Krug, who started several games in 1995 after an injury to first-string signal caller Ron Powlus, dated and ultimately married Sherri Vitale. Krug, now a judge in Florida, found himself called upon to quarterback Notre Dame in the 1996 Orange Bowl Game and threw three touchdown passes in a closely fought 31-26 loss.

"My son-in-law raves about him," Vitale said. "They would have a Mass on the day of the football game for the whole football team and he [Fr. Riehle] would speak and offer the Mass. My son-in-law Thomas just said he was as special as you can get… always optimistic, always energetic."

Vitale said he remembers Fr. Riehle's spirit, enthusiasm, energy and excitement.

Most of all, Vitale recalled Fr. Riehle's "love, I mean a love, for the Lady on the Dome."

Lovable Grump

For a curmudgeon, Fr. Riehle was "very lovable," said "Cappy" Gagnon, who served as a security escort for the football team during road games and stood on the Notre Dame sideline with Fr. Riehle many times.

"Fr. Jim was a grumpy guy, but only in a good way," Gagnon recalled.

As a "huge sports fan," the team chaplain was "not a happy camper" if the Fighting Irish were losing and he felt the officials had blown calls that hurt Notre Dame or if an opposing player did something improper, Gagnon said. Even though he was a priest, Fr. Riehle may have needed to confess to the "sin of anger" or perhaps even using "mild profanity" after a few particularly tough losses, Gagnon added.

We used to joke that he was the only priest at Notre Dame on a golf scholarship, Gagnon said.

But long-standing service to the university did produce some non-monetary benefits for Fr. Riehle.

For example, when Notre Dame's buildings became non-smoking, Fr. Riehle and former Notre Dame President Fr. Hesburgh effectively were "grandfathered" from the prohibition, Gagnon said.

Nobody officially permitted the cigar smoking, Gagnon said. But the "great affection" people at the university had for both men dissuaded anyone from insisting that two legendary leaders at Notre Dame stop doing something they had spent decades enjoying together.

"They each loved a cigar," Gagnon said.

Pays Price

Fr. Riehle's provided "important" and memorable service as an athletics chaplain, said Brian Boulac, who spent 50 years at Notre Dame as a football player, assistant football coach and athletic department administrator.

Although many observers might consider Fr. Riehle lucky for standing next to the head football coach on the sideline during the games, Boulac recalled one time when a football player ran into Fr. Riehle while the priest stood next to the playing field.

"I remember him getting hit once on the sidelines and knocked down," Boulac said. "He was surprised that he got hit. He was very upset and probably cussing under his breath."

Boulac said he told the team chaplain that he needed to watch out when players ran toward him during a game.

That moment demonstrated Fr. Riehle's commitment to Notre Dame athletics. Even as Fr. Riehle's health worsened, he kept serving as an athletic chaplain.

"He was chaplain but also one of the greater supporters," Boulac said. "When I was a young coach, he was omnipresent. It was important for him to be on the sidelines."

Boulac's on-field connection with Notre Dame began when he played tight end on the Fighting Irish football teams during 1959-62, before serving for 18 years in various assistant coaching roles. Fr. Riehle performed the duties of chaplain for Notre Dame football teams that won national championships in 1966, 1973 and 1977 when Boulac was one of the coaches. Bolac also worked with Fr. Riehle for 24 years as an athletic department administrator.

To Boulac, what stands out the most about Fr. Riehle was his willingness to speak his mind on different subjects.

"He would stand behind what he said," Boulac said.

Tantalizing Temptations

Fr. Riehle also understood how temptations could lead someone astray. The priest's personal weakness was not an unusual one for a man. He couldn't seem to resist desserts.

Even though Fr. Riehle and Boulac both battled diabetes, the priest had trouble turning down tempting treats. Boulac noticed the pattern each year when they attended an annual sports banquet and sat next to each other.

One particular local banquet in South Bend took place at a parish hall and the cooks always served sumptuous pie that Fr. Riehle enjoyed.

Boulac had been told by his doctor to give up desserts due to diabetes and figured Fr. Riehle's physician would have advised the priest likewise.

"I kept questioning him about it," Boulac said. "He continued to enjoy the pie even though he knew it was not good for a diabetic."

Doing Double Duty

Jim Fraleigh, a deputy athletic director at Notre Dame and a former executive director of its Monogram Club, originally became acquainted with Fr. Riehle while serving as the student manager of both the football and baseball teams before his graduation in 1988. He returned to the university to work in the athletic department in 1990 and developed a special rapport with Fr. Riehle when they shared adjoining offices for nearly five years at the end of the priest's career at Notre Dame. From that vantage point, Fraleigh learned firsthand about Fr. Riehle's popularity among many former players, coaches and students. Drop-in guests descended upon Fr. Riehle's office in large numbers as if pulled by a magnetic force each Friday during football season.

"He had an ability to really relate to former players," influencing them spiritually, brotherly and fatherly, Fraleigh said. The priest's relationship with each person hinged on what Fr. Riehle thought that particular individual needed. Fr. Riehle put into action his well-honed knack of finding a way to connect with people that he developed as a salesman before becoming a priest.

One of the "geniuses" of Fr. Riehle involved knowing the right "buttons" to push with each athlete, Fraleigh said.

"With the number of people that would come back to see him on any given football weekend, it was very apparent to me that he had such an influence on so many different people in a lot of different ways," Fraleigh said. "Some of them would come in and say, 'You know what, Father? I really appreciate you kicking me in the butt when I needed to be kicked in the butt.' And others would come back and say, 'Father, I appreciate the time you stayed up with me until 3 o'clock in the morning when I had a bad game or didn't play well, or whatever.'"

Revealing Glimpse

As a result of witnessing Fr. Riehle's interactions with people at close range on a daily basis, Fraleigh observed the priest's personality in a variety of situations.

"I got to hear about and observe a lot of different sides that Fr. Riehle maybe didn't show more often, especially toward the end [of his life]," Fraleigh said.

As Fr. Riehle's health deteriorated, he still came to the office as often as four or five times a week until he needed to scale back on his trips into work. He ultimately began working solely out of Holy Cross House where the most senior priests on the Notre Dame campus live. When that happened, Fraleigh began to visit the priest at Holy Cross House. It was a sign of respect that Fr. Riehle appreciated and thanked Fraleigh for extending.

Motivated Manager

Fr. Riehle's legacy involves him boosting dramatically the scholarship fund of Notre Dame's Monogram Club.

"He established that to where it became what it is today," former basketball coach "Digger" Phelps said.

The Monogram Club's members consist of individuals who have earned the university's varsity athletic insignia for athletics or they received an honorary monogram for service to the Notre Dame sports program. The club helps to fund scholarships for members' sons and daughters to attend the university.

Fr. Riehle really was the "heart and soul" of that organization, Phelps said.

Monogram Club Momentum

"Fr. Riehle, at one time, was the Monogram Club," Fraleigh said. The priest grew the Monogram Club into one of the top scholarship-giving organizations at Notre Dame during his tenure as its executive director. The Brennan-Boland-Riehle Scholarship Fund has amassed an endowment of more than $6 million to provide financial aid. Boland, one of the famed Four Horsemen at Notre Dame, is the only varsity letterman among the three honorees. Rev. Brennan was a philosophy professor who preceded Fr. Riehle as Notre Dame's head sports chaplain.

The Brennan-Boland-Riehle Scholarship Awards have provided 295 individual students with financial aid totaling more than $4.4 million through the 2013-2014 school year. That large pool of money is a tribute to Fr. Riehle, who advocated growing the fund to reach a self-sustaining level.

Without Fr. Riehle, there is no way the scholarship fund would have grown past $6.6 million, Fraleigh said.

"There is no other Monogram Club in the country that can claim that," Fraleigh said.

Fr. Riehle served as the day-to-day administrator of the club from 1978 through 2002, when Kevin White, Notre Dame's athletic director at the time, asked Bill Scholl to take the helm. Fr. Riehle became executive director emeritus. Fraleigh succeeded Scholl as executive director in 2004, with Beth Hunter taking the top job in September 2009, and Brant Ust, a former Notre Dame baseball player, doing likewise in March 2014.

Respecting the Reverend

One of Fraleigh's first moves as the club's executive director entailed sitting down with Fr. Riehle and discussing what had happened during the previous two years.

"The Monogram Club was his baby, if you will," Fraleigh said. Fr. Riehle acknowledged that part of him felt as though he had been put out to pasture but he also realized that he no longer physically could serve the club the way that he had previously. Despite recognizing the need for new leadership, Fr. Riehle wished it could have been avoided.

It was a "very difficult transition" for Fr. Riehle, much the way countless others have needed to accept physical limitations and curtail their activities.

"The one thing that I really tried to do every day was to really respect him" as a person, as a priest and as an accomplished administrator, Fraleigh said.

"I made it very clear to him that I was in no way trying to take over what he has done or to change what he's done," Fraleigh said.

Instead, Fraleigh said he wanted to learn from Fr. Riehle and build upon his achievements.

Administrative Acumen

When Fr. Riehle took the reins as the club's executive director, he stepped up fundraising and quickly expanded the club's mission from helping the children of former football players attend Notre Dame to aid the offspring of letter winners from all of the school's sports.

"He did just a fantastic job with that," former hockey coach "Lefty" Smith said. "He made the Monogram Club into one of the most respected groups on campus and generated a tremendous amount of money."

Fr. Riehle invested the money to grow it further. A number of students attended Notre Dame who otherwise would have been unable to do so without financial aid spearheaded by Fr. Riehle.

"From that very first meeting, we got along extremely, extremely well," Fraleigh said. "And then, the toughest part for me was when we redid our offices here and my office became immediately adjacent to his office. That was hard for him, I think, because he really felt like things are changing and things are changing pretty quickly. Not only did it feel different, it now looked different in the form of the office."

However, Fraleigh tried to minimize the potential fallout for Fr. Riehle by promising the priest that he could keep his office. Notre Dame's athletic director supported the decision.

Keep Courtesies

The situation of a once-seemingly indispensable person needing to step aside in any workplace is a knotty transition but gestures of respect help in the adjustment. In a world that often forgoes courtesies that once had been commonplace, Fr. Riehle's shift from heading the Monogram Club to becoming a mentor for its new executive director offers an example of how both sides of a transition can support each other.

"Some of the best times that we had, I think, were not necessarily when he was here at the office but when he was over at Holy Cross House," Fraleigh said. "After lunch every day, he would go into the smoking room that was built for him and Fr. Hesburgh."

Fr. Riehle seemed "happiest" when sitting and smoking his cigar, Fraleigh said.

Along with the cigar smoking came story telling. With advancing age and diabetes taking a toll, Fr. Riehle found contentment in the smoking room at Holy Cross House.

"The best thing that ever happened to our relationship was the ability to just sit in that room and just talk," Fraliegh said.

Respect Past Achievements

Fraleigh said that he "forever" will be grateful to Fr. Riehle not only for accepting him as the Monogram Club's executive director but also for guiding him, "first and foremost, spiritually." If Notre Dame's missions and values stayed paramount, every decision would be "extremely easy," Fraleigh said Fr. Riehle told him.

"I found that to be very true," Fraleigh said.

Fr. Riehle not only was a priest but also an educator, a resource and a friend, Fraleigh said.

Riehle Field

Notre Dame acknowledged Fr. Riehle's contributions to athletics by naming the university's intramural sports field after him.

James Brady, husband of Fr. Riehle's niece "Nan," recalled his brother asking for his grandson Jon to receive a tour of Notre Dame from Fr. Riehle. The grandson lived in North Liberty, Indiana, about 20 miles south of South Bend, and was thinking of attending Notre Dame.

"As part of the tour, we stopped at Riehle Field," Brady said. "I looked at the plaque with Jim's picture and comments of his accomplishments. When I got back in the car I told Jim how nice it was but that I thought they waited until you died to dedicate a field to you. He thought that was pretty funny."

Charitable Chaplain

When Fr. Riehle's mother died, he and his siblings Al and Joan each received a small inheritance. Fr. Riehle invested his portion. A few years before he died, Fr. Riehle sold his stock and divided the proceeds between Holy Cross House and his religious order, Brady said.

Another example of his generosity involved raising money for needy children. Each year that Fr. Riehle spent the winter at Panther Woods in Fort Pierce, Florida, he would conduct a Mass during Easter at the home of one of the residents.

A collection would be taken and Fr. Riehle always matched the funds before giving the money to the Children's Home in South Bend, Brady said.

Indoctrinating 'Uncle Jim'

Fr. Riehle was among the traditionalists who initially had reservations about admitting women to what had been an all-male student population. Ironically, Fr. Riehle's niece, Kathleen Riehle-Valentine, was among the vanguard of female undergraduates who gained admission to Notre Dame and graduated from the university. He may not have been a proponent of the movement but he adapted along with many other people.

"It is true that my Uncle Jim wasn't very fond of the idea of women joining Notre Dame, and I knew it," Riehle-Valentine said. "But what choice did he have? After all, the daughter of his brother would be attending!"

Fr. Hesburgh led the initiative to admit female undergraduates when he was Notre Dame's president. Riehle-Valentine said she felt fortunate to attend Notre Dame during his tenure.

"It was a privilege to be among the first year of female students to attend Notre Dame," Riehle-Valentine said.

Her interest in Notre Dame stemmed from feeling it was "very special" to have an uncle who was a priest and the football team's chaplain, Riehle-Valentine said.

Riehle-Valentine said she probably saw her Uncle Jim on the football field more than anywhere else on campus. Even though she lived in Lyons Hall right across the quadrangle from Pangborn Hall where her uncle was the rector, Riehle-Valentine said she didn't have to "report in" with him.

"I suppose my Dad may have had my uncle check up on me once in a while but I wasn't aware of it," Riehle-Valentine said.

To ensure the women attending Notre Dame at the previously all-male university felt welcome to participate in class, the professors would encourage their input by saying, "now let's hear from the female perspective," Riehle-Valentine recalled. As a "shy" newcomer to the university, Riehle-Valentine said she learned quickly to speak up and share her "female" opinion.

Supported Women's Sports

Despite Fr. Riehle's reputation as a man's man, he became an avid supporter of women's sports at the university when it went coed and started to field varsity athletic teams.

Notre Dame now has one of the top women's sports programs in the country, particularly in basketball and soccer.

One time, Fr. Riehle introduced James Brady and his brother's son Jon to Muffet McGraw, the women's basketball coach, shortly after she led her team to a national championship. Jon was a big fan and Fr. Riehle was happy to tout the women's sports teams.

Naturally, anytime Notre Dame won a national title, Fr. Riehle recognized the benefit to the university's reputation.

A Reunion to Remember

A reunion of hockey players from past Notre Dame club and varsity teams took place during the summer of 2008 and let the attendees see Fr. Riehle a final time. The event lured 100 to 150 former Fighting Irish players back to campus, along with their wives and children.

"It ended up that practically all of them made a visit to Holy Cross House, where Fr. [Riehle] was stationed after he'd had his legs amputated," Smith said. "Then, I picked him up with a special van and took him to the final, formal dinner on the last night of the reunion."

The reunion allowed the former players to talk with the team's inimitable chaplain. It became a "very emotional" evening for Fr. Riehle and the hockey alumni who attended, Smith recalled.

Brian Walsh, the all-time points leader in the history of Notre Dame hockey, attended the reunion and described it as "incredible." The event was "emotionally charged" but also a celebration with Fr. Riehle and Smith, two of the key people involved in the start of Notre Dame's hockey program.

It also was a lesson that life moves on, since Fr. Riehle's days on Earth were waning. Jeff Jackson, the hockey coach Notre Dame hired from outside of the university in May 2005, had begun achieving his own success, Walsh said.

Even though Fr. Riehle died just weeks later, the value of his assistance to others might last for generations.

Greatest Gift?

For the Gorman family, Fr. Riehle personally intervened to provide the gift of a Notre Dame education to a deserving but financially needy student and made a classic American success story possible. Steve Gorman seized the chance, graduated from Notre Dame and later dental school, and watched his daughter Emily follow him to the university where she earned her own degree in 2012.

That story "stands out as much as anything" that Fr. Riehle did, Smith said.

Final Farewell

Dr. Gorman had a last chance to meet with Fr. Riehle when the dentist's daughter became a Notre Dame freshman in 2008. Unlike when Steve Gorman needed to drive himself to Notre Dame for his freshman year, he escorted his daughter there and discovered a "real re-connection" with the university and Fr. Riehle.

In his heyday, Fr. Riehle resembled the actor Lee J. Cobb, who was nominated for an Academy Award twice for best actor in a supporting role.

"The image I remember most of him is on the sidelines at the football games," Dr. Gorman said.

But Dr. Gorman learned from Smith upon returning to campus that Fr. Riehle's health was failing. Dr. Gorman had talked about Fr. Riehle and his importance throughout his daughter's life, so both of them were interested in seeing the ailing priest.

"At first, he did not recognize me but he later did," Dr. Gorman said.

When Fr. Riehle realized it was the same Steve Gorman he had helped to complete his Notre Dame degree, the elderly priest perked up.

"I pushed his wheelchair to the dining table," Dr. Gorman said. "Before I left, I got teary eyed."

Death-Defying Blessing

The dentist's eyes moistened as he thanked the priest for all that he had done to assist him. But it became apparent that the dying clergyman wanted to help one last time.

"He told me to come over, kneel by him and he blessed me," Dr. Gorman said. "My daughter observed this. It was a special moment for me with him and for her with me."

It may well have marked the last blessing or one of the last blessings that Fr. Riehle was able to give anyone before his death.

Just weeks later, Fr. Riehle took his last breath. Dr. Gorman was among the attendees at the funeral Mass held at the Basilica of the Sacred Heart on Notre Dame's campus. Alongside the dentist sat his daughter, who had a chance to see firsthand Fr. Riehle's powerful influence on her father and a large number of other people who attended the funeral and spoke of the clergyman's positive effect on their lives. The funeral Mass became another bonding experience for the father and the daughter.

"It was special for my daughter to be with me at the funeral," Dr. Gorman said.

The funeral was an emotion-filled day for the father and the daughter, since both realized that neither would have been able to attend Notre Dame without Fr. Riehle's assistance. The father, who lived off of public assistance as a child, may not have become a successful professional otherwise. It also is questionable whether she then would have been as interested and as committed to one day attending the school, without Fr. Riehle's intervention.

Tragic Turn

At Fr Riehle's funeral, Fr. Hesburgh recalled needing to tell the first-year student that his father died and learning Jim Riehle did not have a cent to return home for the funeral. Word of his plight spread quickly to others.

"It didn't take more than 10 minutes to gather the funds from their poor resources to send Jim along his way," Fr. Hesburgh recalled.

Years later, Jim Riehle joined a number of other former Badin Hall residents in becoming priests, Fr. Hesburgh said.

Inspiring Eulogy

"It was sad how he died," Phelps said. "He lost one leg when diabetes got to him, and then he lost the second leg. Then he passed on."

But Fr. Riehle likely would not want people to focus on the way he died, but rather how he lived. It is in living fully that we can make the biggest difference for others, as well as to enhance the meaning of our own lives.

"This is not as sad as it might be because it is filled with happy memories of a wonderful priest who lived in our midst, who worked in our midst and who loved all of you so much in his own quiet way," Fr. Hesburgh said during his eulogy for Fr. Riehle.

Virtually everybody seemed to love Fr. Riehle, Fr. Hesburgh said. Despite Fr. Riehle's "stern side" to his nature, he had a genuine love for the students, Fr. Hesburgh added.

"He could always be counted on," Fr. Hesburgh said.

Dick Riehle said his cousin Fr. Riehle once told him, "Dying and going to heaven is good but it can't be any better than being here at Notre Dame."

Faithful Friends

A reflection of his devotion to others was exhibited at Fr. Riehle's funeral Mass when more than 70 priests set aside other duties to send him on his journey toward eternity, Fr. Hesburgh said. Rather than consider the funeral a time of sadness, it instead afforded an opportunity to share recollections about his life.

One of his most enduring influences upon many Notre Dame students took place when he served as rector at then newly build Pangborn Hall, following a short stint as rector at Sorin Hall, the first dormitory at the university.

"Jim left a lasting impression at Pangborn Hall, which is now a women's hall," Fr. Hesburgh said. "In those first decades of young men coming here to study as he did, he was, indeed, a father to many of them."

Gorman's Gift

The only time Emily Gorman was able to meet Fr. Riehle occurred when her dad took her with him to visit the priest on the same weekend that she moved into her room as a first-year student at Pangborn Hall.

"My dad thought it was important for both of us to go and see him [Fr. Riehle], because my dad hadn't seen him in a great number of years," Emily said. Her father also wanted his daughter to meet Fr. Riehle, since the priest had been "so important" to her dad's ultimate graduation from Notre Dame, she added.

Ever since she can remember, Emily said when her dad discussed his Notre Dame years, he mentioned Fr. Riehle and the key role that the priest played for him.

"I had previously known about the relationship that they'd had, but just seeing it was really special," Emily said. "It was really perfect timing," she said, especially since the priest's health was fading quickly and he would be on his death bed within weeks. If the visit had been delayed just one semester, Emily would have missed the chance to meet the priest who had become her father's personal advocate at Notre Dame.

Interested in Others

Fr. Riehle paid special attention to Emily during her visit with him and seemed delighted that she was attending Notre Dame, she recalled. The priest asked about what she wanted to do with her life.

"I thought that was very telling of his character, just being so interested in me and asking me more than just the basics of, How did I like Notre Dame," Emily recalled.

"He got quite a kick out of the fact that I was living in Pangborn Hall," the same dormitory where he father lived for three years when Fr. Riehle was the rector.

"We had that in common," Emily said.

The most powerful moment of the meeting may have been when Fr. Riehle blessed her kneeling father in front of her.

"It was the most emotion that I've probably ever seen in my dad," Emily said. "It was just a really special moment."

It was clear to Emily that her father appreciated the chance to visit Fr. Riehle, who was the one person at Notre Dame who refused to let finances determine whether a then-aspiring dentist could remain at the university and complete his degree. It was Fr. Riehle who told the student that he was "important" and was going to stay, Emily said.

Parental Presence

Without Fr. Riehle, Emily said she never would have become a student at Notre Dame and her dad never would have been able to stay at the university to finish his degree decades earlier.

When a lack of finances threatened to force Emily's father out of Notre Dame, Fr. Riehle is the one who stated, "'No, wait a minute. This is not right,'" she said.

"He did so much for my dad," Emily said about Fr. Riehle.

Emily graduated from Notre Dame summa cum laude in 2012 with a double major in business and Spanish.

She reflected upon how essential Fr. Riehle was to her dad, whose own father and step-father gave little or no support to their son.

"I've always had two parents who were there for me," Emily said.

At a critical point in her father's life, Fr. Riehle filled that parental role.

"It definitely enabled my dad to stay at Notre Dame," Emily said. "He had so much help from Fr. Riehle."

After hearing stories about Fr. Riehle's role to assist her dad throughout her life and learning more about him by attending the funeral, Emily said she felt like she knew the priest much better than by just meeting him once.

Favorite Fan

Fr. Riehle also helped people who were special in other ways. One of Notre Dame's biggest fans might be Keith Penrod, who did not let cerebral palsy and the need to use a wheelchair stop him from attending sporting events for more than three decades. In honor of his loyalty, he has received game balls from coaches for cheering unfailingly for the school's teams.

"Reels would always take care of him, and he'd always be around the bench for basketball," Phelps said.

"When you think of Notre Dame and you think of priests, Fr. Riehle is really right up there with what makes Notre Dame so special," Phelps said.

Stoic Dinner Companion

"I had the honor of sitting next to him at meals during these past years at Holy Cross House," Fr. Hesburgh said. "And, it was easy to see how his illness was catching up with him and testing his spirit, and his courage."

During that time, one thing after another went wrong health-wise for Fr. Riehle. He first lost one leg to diabetes, then the other.

"He continued in a wheel chair to show up for meals each day," Fr. Hesburgh said. "He took part in the table talk. He always had a kind of grim humor that we all enjoyed."

Fr. Riehle tried to accept the burdens of his failing health without letting the various afflictions prevent him from making the best of his diminishing life.

"He didn't complain," Fr. Hesburgh said. "He didn't growl, which he could do quite easily, I might say. He didn't say all of it was bad. He knew it was the will of God and he accepted it."

The night before he died, a long line of people visited during his final hours. Fr. Riehle easily could have lamented many things that were going awry, but he never did, Fr. Hesburgh said.

"He didn't gripe when he couldn't play golf anymore because of his legs," Fr. Hesburgh said. "He didn't gripe when he was confined to a wheelchair, which was a terrible penance for one who loved sports and activity. He didn't gripe when it pained him, as it did increasingly as the days went by. I think he has given all of us, priests and friends, an example of what a Christian life is when lived fully and completely."

Carried Big Stick

"He was enamored by the wonderful tradition of football, basketball and other sports here," Fr. Hesburgh said. "He was himself a first-class hockey player, even though some would say that putting a stick in the hands of Jim Riehle was a dangerous thing to do."

The greatest contributions of Fr. Riehle did not come as a competitive athlete but as a faithful adviser and spiritual guide to students, professors, coaches and others.

Fr. Riehle became "the greatest friend" for Notre Dame athletes, Fr. Hesburgh said. He accompanied the university's teams to games, both home and away, as well as distributed hundreds of medals of "Our Lady" to the athletes before they went out to compete for Notre Dame, Hesburgh added.

It was no idle praise when Fr. Hesburgh, Notre Dame's esteemed former president, ranked Fr. Riehle among the university's most valuable people, even though the one-time sports chaplain served in the background and never sought attention.

"It's not easy to adequately say what a man has done in his life, but I can tell you with sincerity that he was one of the great ones here in a quiet way," Fr. Hesburgh said. "He did what needed doing, and he did it quietly and well. He was there when student-athletes needed him. And, he was there with firmness and with love; both of those went together in his life."

Fr. Riehle likely would have stayed true to form if he was watching his own funeral Mass by suggesting that the eulogy be kept brief, Fr. Hesburgh said.

"I think about now I can hear Jim saying to me in his gruff voice, 'That's about enough, Ted, I think you've overdone it already and you don't need to do anymore.' So I won't."

Fr. Hesburgh concluded his eulogy of Fr. Riehle with a simple prayer that the former university president said was as old as the church itself: "Eternal rest, grant onto him, O Lord. Let perpetual light shine upon him. May he rest in peace."

Respected by Regis

Television personality Regis Philbin, a Notre Dame alumnus and benefactor, singled out Fr. Riehle's enthusiasm along the sidelines at football games as one of his lasting memories of the chaplain. In turn, Fr. Riehle's largely unknown acumen with finances and figures let him remember the exact amount of a major contribution from Philbin for a new performing arts center at Notre Dame.

Whether giving special attention to fans such as Penrod or welcoming media personalities such as Philbin, Fr. Riehle played a key role at Notre Dame for four action-packed decades. Regardless of one's allegiance to that university or another one, Fr. Riehle understood the value of looking beyond our differences and connecting with people, enjoying the blessings of a given moment and helping others do likewise. Institutions consist of people and Fr. Riehle certainly brought his unique talents to one that French priests built in central Indiana and named after the mother of Christ.

Philbin summed up Fr. Riehle's service and significance to the university in the following way, "He is Notre Dame."

CONCLUSION

A clergyman's life should not be measured in mighty deeds or personal achievements that are considered traditional signs of success in the secular world. The accumulation of money, valuable possessions and fame are not the goals of someone such as Fr. Riehle. He gained satisfaction from serving the Lord and helping others do likewise, whatever their religious beliefs or their personal callings in life.

Many people would describe Fr. Riehle as one of the best advisers they have known. Notre Dame players and coaches of varying religious views found Fr. Riehle to be a source of inspiration and spiritual strength, especially during times of immense stress. Students, whether athletes or not, benefitted from his fatherly influence, even if he sometimes showed a stern side to his personality. Yet others remarked about how Fr. Riehle's presence in their lives gave them needed discipline to stay focused on their goals and the fulfillment of their potential.

For Fr. Riehle, his treasure would be the everlasting life that Christ promised awaits us in the heavenly kingdom of the Lord. Fr. Riehle would not want that ultimate victory just for himself but for the rest of us, too. In life, he personally ministered to the needs of those he met who sought to find heightened meaning in their own lives and the motivation to pursue it. In death, his memory offers a legacy of a man of God who humbly tried to improve the condition of others in ways that the rest of us can try to emulate. Fr. Riehle's lasting lessons for life offer a template to give each of us a sense of purpose and an invitation to provide faithful service to others on our personal paths to happiness.

INDEX

Printed in the USA
CPSIA information can be obtained
at www.ICGtesting.com
LVHW011429280624
784231LV00003B/38

9 781498 406901